Meaningful Learning in the Church

by Donald M. Joy

Light and Life Press
999 College Avenue
Winona Lake, Indiana 46590

Printed in the United States of America
Published by Light and Life Press, Winona Lake, Indiana 46590

Second printing 1974
Third printing 1977
Fourth printing 1980
Fifth printing 1984
Revised 1989

Library of Congress Catalogue Card Number: 72-80801

ISBN 0-89367-019-7

To my wife, Robbie, constant companion
in education
Met in a library,
Wed during college,
Fellow teacher in school,
Co-teacher at church,
Graduate school colleague,
First counsel in ideas,
Partner in nurture
Of two charming sons.

Contents

The concept "Christian"
The principle: "A Christian is . . . "
Looking back from principle to facts

Programmed instruction in the church
"Live curriculum" for an adult elective
A formula for meaningful teaching

Introduction

In the late 1960s, carrying denominational and some wider responsibilities for Sunday school curriculum publications, I went in search of graduate training. I wanted it to be up-to-date specifically on issues of learning and teaching. Since I held a basic graduate divinity degree from Asbury Theological Seminary (1954) and an education degree from Southern Methodist University (1960), I wanted specific curriculum development help.

The field quickly narrowed. Two factors shook down the options: (1) Graduate schools of theology, including the prestigious Ivy League schools, were only marketing "warmed over" teaching that was clearly about three generations from current established findings. (2) Only the great, heavily funded "doctoral research" universities seemed to have the specialization I wanted.

The time lag was understandable. The three generations of research lapse was clearly related to (a) teaching faculty working out of their graduate school bag of knowledge, and (b) their lack of participation in ongoing research. So the field narrowed, in 1965, to three universities with curriculum development research programs and faculties: Columbia in New York, University of Chicago, and Indiana University.

Education textbooks tend to be among the most abstract, impenetrable literature on earth. Usually this is a sign that a book is simply "warmed-over, second-hand stuff." Occasionally it is because an author has abstracted--boiled down--mountains of evidence into technical language.

With the help of Dr. Catherine Stonehouse, who was, in 1969, a new and gifted member of the editorial staff I managed, this book should be neither "abstract" nor technical. The manuscript came to her full of educational jargon, an echo of my research and final seminar phase at Indiana University. Today Dr. Stonehouse is my colleague and is shaping the next generation of curriculum specialists in many denominations who depend on Asbury Seminary for developing their leaders.

I offer *Meaningful Learning in the Church* to you as a book about the educational mission of the church. I wrote it out of convictions which emerged during my doctoral program and under the summons of my colleagues in the multi-denominational curriculum development group with whom I was working in the late sixties. I have revised the book now, on the eve of the nineties, with a sense that our mission remains remarkably similar to that of more than twenty years ago. In some cases my predictions have come true, so I have extended the prophetic lines a bit.

Still, Christian education textbooks coming out of the seminaries remain fairly ingrown, and consist of secondhand fabric, showing little awareness of educational insights about *how* people learn. This is all the more a puzzle because the Judeo-Christian line of thought has apparently spawned most of the grand ideas of the Western world. The church might be looked upon as the parent of modern education, which is pushing back the frontiers of knowledge as we fulfill our destiny as managers or dominion-holders of this planet. For hundreds of years God used different methods to reveal himself to people in order to transform them, but the ultimate "curriculum" for transformation culminated in the Incarnation of God in Jesus Christ.

It is important for us to continue to ask serious questions about our work in the churches. We need to take an introspective look, for example, at Christian education, with special attention to whether it is truly *Christian* in its goals, techniques, and content. Ultimately, however, an even larger question must be faced: Is Christian education really *education*? If humans are God's creation, then their capacity for learning and their ways of knowing are appropriate concerns for Christian educators. It would be the grandest irony of all time if ever it even seemed that we were saying, "We do not care *how* humans learn; we know *what* we want to teach!"

The first conviction giving rise to this book, then, is this: *Humans are specially endowed creatures with a capacity to know and to learn. If they are to be well served by the church, we must be attentive to the emerging strategies of learning.*

Closely related to this basic conviction is my belief

that the future of humanity will be shaped by religious ideas which command respect. In the midst of what is often called a secular society, one of America's foremost educators has openly appealed for someone to articulate a set of commanding "myths" which will organize the human race around meaningful and ennobling goals. He speaks as a secularist, but also as a realist. He reminds us that the future of humanity is bleak and probably very short unless the human race is caught by some elevating vision that will spur us to creative action and draw us toward a goal that makes the future worthwhile. The root disease of our age is probably not our ghetto rot, our sexual promiscuity with its deadly diseases, or our drug addiction, but the loss of a clear sense of human destiny that sees ourselves and every other person as possessing immeasurable worth. The tragedies into which we pour millions of essential dollars to relieve pain and to cancel the effects of evil are, themselves, only *symptoms* of the deeper disease: our loss of a sense of identity and dignity as humans.

Norman Cousins, then editor of *Saturday Review,* reminded us all, in the wake of the U.S. Surgeon General's report on smoking, that the enlightened person who continues to smoke is a symbol of what he called "the danger beyond smoking." That danger is that life may have lost its meaning: "What difference does five or ten years make?"

The second conviction on which this book rests is this: *The grand ideas of the Christian faith as expressed in Holy Scripture and in the person of Jesus Christ concerning the nature of humanity, the world,*

God, sin, and salvation constitute the most ennobling and driving vision ever entertained in the mind of beings on this planet. It remains for those of us who are possessed by this faith and who are its custodians to communicate it meaningfully to everyone who can be brought under its influence.

I am increasingly strengthened in my belief that the lay-volunteer teaching staff in the church may well be its most powerful arm of influence in the world. In taking this position I stand apart from an impressive panel of Christian education specialists who would call for the church to employ professional educators in this technological and sophisticated age.

I have not come to my position on lay-volunteer leadership easily and have, in fact, made every effort to sharpen my own Christian education skills. My continuing quest for excellence may place me outside the lay-volunteer class, but if it does, it also equips me to make certain observations which are rooted both in my life-long experience and in what I see today.

The lay-volunteer teacher who is a warmhearted Christian, for example, is a living "incarnation" of God in the world. That person may fracture the English language or draw a poor diagram, but here is living proof that Jesus Christ makes a difference in a person's attitudes, way of life, and goals. Lesson writers can help the lay volunteer understand the phenomenon of adolescence or the reasonable expectations for young children. They can structure the session plan for maximum learning. But a small staff of professional, Christian educators charged with teaching everyone in the church could never create compelling evidence that God lives in and works through ordinary people who work in shops and kitchens in a particular village or city. Every exploding congregation will be likely to employ an education minister who is a specialist. But the specialist is always a facilitator, a teaching coach. And the congregation's professional leaders are surely in a unique position to provide both the lay training that is essential through apprenticeships and special intensive seminars, and also to provide significant honor and reward to the volunteers.

Those who urge us to employ Christian education specialists to handle all church classes or who insist that we send all volunteers away for graduate training seem to suggest that our structures of knowledge are complicated and difficult to understand and teach. It could be argued, however, that just the opposite is true; the main lines of knowledge possesssed by the church are fairly simple, but the values, concepts, and attitudes treasured by the church are hopelessly complex. Now if our chief resource is in these complex areas, we must admit that they are virtually impossible to *explain;* at the same time we must also affirm that they are easy to *demonstrate*--to "flesh out" in real life as Jesus Christ lives through a transformed person. What we need, then, is not a panel of educational technicians, but a staff of workshop leaders and laboratory partners to turn loose with classes of students who may then be exposed to a distinctive set of concepts, values, and attitudes.

What is more, the intricate theories spun from careful educational research have a ring of truth and simplicity that makes it plausible for a sensitive lay teacher to be an effective witness. Christianity has taken a frank and realistic view of humanity; it has obligated itself to work with people as they are to help them become the people they were created to be. Effective teaching, then, amounts only to "working with the grain" written into humanity at Creation and by our accumulated history. Shop foremen, homemakers, doctors, and schoolteachers are all able to teach their own infants the most complicated matters--language and social and cultural values and behaviors. They are all, likewise, first-class candidates to teach the concepts, values, and attitudes of Christianity.

The ideas presented in this book are manageable by any alert adult. They represent the kinds of knowledge that come from technical fields which throw light upon the nature of learning. Teachers should expect to find insights from tips scattered through the teaching-learning suggestions in the church curriculum guide and in the teacher-training services of their local congregation. What neither curriculum materials nor professional staff can do is relate to typical people in a specific cultural setting. That task can be done only as the concepts, values, and attitudes of the Christ-life come alive in the native-speaking lay volunteer.

The third conviction, then, is this: *The most convincing specimen of the power of Jesus Christ in the world is the typical lay-volunteer teacher, who may need abundant help in making teaching effective, but who brings to the teaching task--by virtue of sheer commitment to Christ--a complex set of skills for communicating Christian concepts, values, and attitudes.*

The chapters which follow rest on these affirmations and amplify them. It will become obvious that I am dependent on a large number of people whose insights and imaginations I have brought to bear upon the task of Christian education in the local church.

I would never have written this book--it would have turned out to be something violently different!-- but for the counsel of Shirley H. Engle and William Lynch and the direction my inquiry took at Indiana University. It was my colleagues in the development of the multi-denominational Aldersgate Graded Curriculum who actually urged me to write: Paul Kindschi and Armor Peisker of the Wesleyan Church, Albert Harper of the Church of the Nazarene, and Almon White of the Evangelical Friends Alliance.

Last of all, but they had significant influence on the actual shape the ideas took, I am indebted to the five members of the Protestant Religious Education team with whom I traveled for six weeks throughout the United States Air Force European Command early in 1968: Thomas Potter, Jr., of the Methodist Publishing House; Findley B. Edge, Christian education professor from Southern Baptist Seminary in Louisville, Kentucky; James Nisbet of the Board of Christian Education of the Presbyterian Church in the United States; Robert L. Thomas, parish priest, All Saints Episcopal Church in Norton, Virginia; and the late Norman Langholz, who served as coordinator of field services in the division of parish education in the American Lutheran Church.

Meaningful Learning in the Church has served for twenty years as a "primer" in Christian education. Its reception around the world on United States Military Bases in Chapel ministry training has extended my 1968 service stint with the USAF in Europe in Chapel training conferences. But the primer continues to find its way into colleges and universities where Christian education concentrations flourish. My own students sing its praises as one of the rare books "anybody could understand"!

"What would you revise, if we took the book back to press again?" the publisher asked. I have been using and reading responses to this book now for eighteen years in a graduate course entitled "The Ministry of Teaching." "Not much," I replied. While I have never really stopped thinking about, researching, and writing about teaching during the last twenty years, I have a sense that *Meaningful Learning in the Church* is in some sense the foundation for everything else I have said or written. My chapters on the importance of networks in relationships and on "Parents and Children: For Each Other" in *Bonding: Relationships in the Image of God* are really grounded here. So also is my entire discussion of "God's First Curriculum" which is heavily woven through *Parents, Kids, and Sexual Integrity.* And in *Walk On! Let God Make You Whole and Holy,* the concept of experience as God's agenda for spiritual formation is under scrutiny as the deeper curriculum God is using for us in daily experiences of ecstacy and pain.

So when the publisher switched on the green light for this second edition for another round of printings to serve the future, I said an easy "Yes." I have determined to leave the text largely unchanged except for upgrading language to my new sensitivities and expanding two or three research foundations for key concepts I have offered.

I am ready to write an entirely new book, not to replace this primer, but to add a parallel foundational exploration of "meaningful teaching in the church." The publisher has said "Yes" to that aspiration, too.

Donald M. Joy, Ph. D.
Professor of Human Development
Ray and Mary Jo West Chair of Christian Education
Asbury Theological Seminary
Wilmore, Kentucky 40390
May, 1989

1

What's Going On in Sunday School?

Television cameras played back and forth from the quizmaster to a soundproof booth, where a handsome young Columbia University instructor perspired and reached into the depths of his memory to dredge up the answers to complicated questions. It gave you a good feeling to watch Charles Van Doren. Here was a fellow who remembered all of those things you had forgotten since you passed your last test in college--or in high school.

Van Doren eventually won $129,000 on the television quiz show "Twenty-One." He was great. Then a grand jury began asking questions. At first, Van Doren testified that he had never received answers to questions in advance of a quiz. Then, on October 17, 1960, he was arrested on charges of perjury. It had been discovered that he had, indeed, received not only answers but also questions in advance.

Most of us were a little sad. Van Doren had turned out to be dishonest. But secretly we had hoped that humans were capable of storing large quantities of factual material for immediate recall--even if only college professors could do it. Now it began to look as if the old adage was more right than wrong: "Educa-

tion is what you have left when you have forgotten everything that you learned."

Sunday school and facts

Many people today are asking questions about what children are learning in Sunday school. There have been some bright people trying to find out. The typical "test" requires one to do the Van Doren trick --dredge factual information:

Who preached on the day of Pentecost?
Name four of the twelve apostles.
Who used a tent peg to kill whom?
Name two kings of Israel.

The results of such tests are consistently terrifying. One survey studied seventeen Baptist churches in Kentucky. Questions were described as purely factual. Churches were classified as urban or rural. Urban churches were divided into high income, middle income, and low income social classes. The test had fifty questions.

Results? The average score was 16.57, or about 33 percent accuracy. We are not told how it was determined that these were fifty things a competent Baptist ought to know, but if they were fifty valid items, then 33 percent would suggest that they flunked. Here are two typical questions, each of them missed by almost two-thirds of those tested:

Jesus said the greatest in the kingdom of heaven

Jesus said the greatest in the kingdom of heaven would be
- (a) the servant of all
- (b) poor
- (c) pure in heart

On the day of Pentecost 3,000 were added to the church after
- (a) Peter
- (b) Paul
- (c) John preached

With a possible score of 50, the adult average was 20.66. The mean for young people was 16.39. Intermediates averaged 12.64, and juniors 5.81.[1]

No doubt some pastors would lose sleep if they thought long on the fact that two-thirds of their pew holders could neither name half of the twelve apostles nor list the books of the Pentateuch. On the other hand, some would raise the question, "What facts must one be able to feed back to prove he is a competent Christian, anyway?" They could further nettle us: "If you don't know what you are trying to teach, then how can you possibly construct a test to see whether you have taught it?"

One investigator set about to test the validity of asking purely factual questions long after study has been finished. He tested adults who were teaching in nine Sunday schools. Seven purely factual questions were given to staff members chosen at random. Since the staffs were all educated in United States public schools, the questions were drawn from facts they would have covered--some of them repeatedly--in the course of their first twelve years of school. Besides, since twelve years of school equals 15,120 hours of education, it seemed more reasonable to expect them to remember facts from that experience than from Sunday school, where one adds up only about a first grade time investment after twenty-four years of attendance.

Here are the seven items used:

1. Name two kings of the Holy Roman Empire.
2. Who was the American patriot who rode into Concord to warn the villagers that the British were coming?
3. Name four consecutive presidents of the United States, including Abraham Lincoln.
4. Give the sense of the nineteenth amendment.
5. Name the three world powers commonly referred to, during World War II, as "The Axis."
6. Name three present states in the United States across which the Chisholm Trail ran.
7. During whose administration was the Louisiana Territory purchased?[2]

There were four correct answers given during the nine times the quiz was administered. The correct responses amounted to an astounding 6.3 percent. With results like that, one could draw any one of several conclusions: (1) History teachers are a colossal failure in U.S. public education. They should all be disciplined or fired, or both. (2) The people polled in the survey were a "bad batch" and didn't reflect the real state of adult Americans' retention of historical facts. (3) The test covered purely factual items that have little abiding significance in the lives of the people tested, and may, in fact, have been constructed by a teacher as a trick exam.

Are Sunday school teachers failures?

Results such as those from the Kentucky Baptist survey mentioned above usually lead to a conclusion that Sunday school teachers are failures. The recommendation which inevitably follows is "We must have better teacher training." More specifically, the accusation is that these teachers do not "know the Bible." If they did, the argument goes, it would naturally follow that their students would overflow with information that they had absorbed from the Sunday school teachers.[3]

Before we can say whether Sunday school teachers are failures, we must know what they are supposed to be doing. The mounting evidence suggests that they are not fixing facts in the minds of students for long-range memory. The next question to ask might be "Are persons changed by their exposure to Christian facts?" That is, "When they have forgotten all of the facts they learned, does anything remain that marks them as products of Christian nurture in the Sunday school?" Unfortunately, the researchers have rarely tried to measure the more complicated kinds of learning that might remain beyond the purely factual material.

More than facts

Pick up any publisher's curriculum samples and scan the contents. The same names are there: Adam, Abraham, Joseph, Moses, David, John the Baptist, Jesus, Peter, Paul, John. The same geographic details are laid out. Essentially the same chronology is set forth. One could assume that facts is all there is to Sunday school, and that they are about the same in any curriculum. But suppose that the purely factual stuff of which Sunday school curriculum seems to be made is really only the building material, which must be worked and shaped into something bigger than the sum of its parts.

Suppose that I asked you the significance of the concept of women's rights in American political and social life. Would that mean any more to you than if I were to ask you to give the sense of the nineteenth amendment or to explain equal rights? Could you comment on the relationship between taxation and representation as a concept in United States political history? The "big idea," or the concept, is the lasting contribution education makes to people.

In the sea of Bible facts in which we immerse our young and ourselves, are there some big ideas which are taking shape? Are teachers in conversation with students in such a way that life-shaping concepts are forming about

1. The nature of God
2. The nature of humanity
3. Sin

4. Salvation
5. The world

These, you see, are more than facts. But if these grand ideas are to be shaped in peoples' minds, they must be carefully formed by working through a sea of facts. Every congregation that has a clear message to offer to the world has a particular set of these concepts to share. Any denomination that takes its mission seriously makes every effort to develop those distinctive concepts in the minds of people to whom it ministers. Indeed, one could ask whether a church deserves to exist if it has no distinctive and crucial word of hope to share with its world. That message of hope will be clearly seen in the teachings about God, humanity, sin, salvation, and the world.[4] Indeed, one could ask whether there are any facts to be learned in the church that cannot be fitted into these master concepts.

Is knowledge virtue?

We have long suspected that the Christian faith is contagious--"better caught than taught." In the Sunday school we have an unparalleled opportunity to spread the contagion of our faith. Deeply committed adults are scattered among the young and throughout adult groups. Groups are small enough that anyone may participate in conversations about the Christian faith.

This contagion that draws people to Jesus and to

personal renewal through the grace of God is not only the most effective means for reaching the lost and enlarging the church; it may be the only means. Christian education has never been able, by instruction alone, to evangelize the world. Notice that the first-century Christians reached their world by introducing people to three life-changing forces:

1. The person of Jesus Christ
2. Transforming new birth
3. The written Scriptures

Indeed, New Testament literature was not available for several generations. The preaching of the gospel was perhaps an equivalent of Scripture, but it focused upon bringing people immediately face to face with Jesus and to repentance and faith in response to the grace of God.

Today's church works with the same three forces. We tend, however, to have altered the order in which a person meets them. This tends to be today's order:

1. The written Scriptures
2. Transforming new birth
3. The body of Christ

First-century Christians seem to have spread their faith by first bringing pagans into a gracious acquaintance with Jesus. This acquaintance then led to their personal new birth. Finally, they were indoctrinated with Christian beliefs--in which role Holy Scripture was used.

We, in contrast, seem to imagine that if we can begin with instruction, we can lead a person to conversion. Finally, we can admit the convert into the magnetic fellowship of believers--the body of Christ. We work in exactly reverse order from the first century. We fail to see that the church, if it is really the body of Christ, is the magnetic force in the world to which frustrated and lonely persons are most likely to be drawn--just as they were drawn to our Lord. The new birth can be logically expected to follow that drawing. And the authenticity of a person's conversion may not often seem to bear any direct correlation to the length of the instruction period. It could even be demonstrated that some persons seem to pass a point of no return if their educational exposure drags on and on without personal response to the offered grace of Jesus. It may be that our bombardment of new recruits and our own children with the facts and implications of discipleship prior to their commitment may often immunize them against radical conversion. Our education that precedes evangelism must somehow meet the awakening needs and interests of the uncommitted without overexposing them to the necessary mechanics and disciplines of mature Christian practice and *faith*. It will be a serious error if we suppose that education alone will do the work of the church. When we have succeeded in getting a person to Sunday school, we have not placed the new recruit on a magic carpet that will automatically land him on his feet before the minister, affirming personal faith in Christ and accepting membership in the church.

Our assumption with our children and with new

recruits might be valid if it were true that "to know is to do." The terrifying fact evident everywhere about us, however, is that there is not always a high correlation between knowledge and virtue--between facts and character. There is a legend to the effect that the late Nikita Khrushchev, Russian head of state, memorized the entire Four Gospels as a young boy. He then allegedly recited them nonstop for his vicar. Afterward he is said to have turned, fled from his church, climbed through a fence into a field, and consumed on the spot the candy which he had received as a prize.

The gift of new life

How can the church, through its teaching ministry, or at least with the help of it, breathe into its young and into its new recruits the "breath of life"? What is the relationship of the witness of the church to its teaching? What are the relationships of biblical and historical facts to the big ideas that lift and nourish and remain after specific facts have been forgotten? That is, how are concepts formed? Indeed, how do humans learn? How do we develop skill in making decisions?

These are questions which we must explore together, not only because the effectiveness of the church in the world is at stake, but because we stand at the frontiers of discovery--only now are we beginning to understand how learning occurs.

2

Focus on People

Look in on any Sunday school class in your church. There they sit. What brought them to church today? What thoughts are in their minds? Take a sample:

I'm sleepy. Why didn't I go to bed earlier?
I wonder why Susie isn't here yet.
Sunday school ... like vitamins ... good for me.
He's really cool!
I'm comfortable. Every Sunday of my life I'm here.
We're going to the lake after church.
Dad would be pleased I'm here. May he rest in peace.
My feet hurt.
I'd better get that raise next week!
Should I go to night school?
I wonder whether Dad is home yet.
What's with me? Life doesn't stack up much.
I wish he would straighten his tie.
Lord Jesus, open my mind, enlighten my life.
I'm so lonely. I wonder if anyone will speak to me.

Bible-centered Sunday school

There has sometimes been debate on whether there should be Bible-centered teaching or student-centered teaching in the church. That argument should probably be abandoned in favor of the ultimate question: What was the focus of Jesus' teaching? Even with the ultimate question defined, we might fail to go to Jesus Christ himself to learn. Most of us imagine that we know what is Christian about Christian education.

When we leaf through the pages of the Gospels looking for strategies Jesus used, there are some patterns of action which seem to characterize His ministry. Those actions are clearly rooted in His perfect understanding of human beings; Jesus knew people as individuals. Jesus saw human beings as having great value, worthy of His intimate concern, part of His personal responsibility. If we would educate, we must understand human beings and the ways they respond to ideas and concepts--how they learn. If we regard them merely as a distant crowd of faceless and nameless beings whose bodies need to be counted both in our church and in heaven, we are not getting seriously involved with them. If we seek to imitate the method of Jesus without acquiring His deep sense of understanding for people, we will find ourselves engaged in "Christian education" that is not Christian.

On the other hand, in the glow of our personal relationship to Christ, we may be driven by a spontaneous and deep affection for others. But if we have no

understanding of how to effectively show that con-
cern--if we have not taken the trouble to learn about
basic human needs--we can never hope to achieve
any excellence in our teaching. We will be caught with
a "Christian education" which is not education.

If Christian education is to be both Christian and
education, we must learn from Jesus on both dimensions. He knew people as no one had ever known them
before. It was as if the master designer of an invention
had suddenly walked into the shop where his best-
crafted machine was grinding away with bent and
twisted parts. But, having been involved with us from
our creation, Jesus also knew how to relate to us; how
to remold us into the image of our original selves--
into His own image.

Jesus, the teacher

The overwhelming impression one gets of Jesus is
that He was able to see things from every person's
point of view. Because of this understanding He was
able to meet the individual at the level of his immediate needs (even desires) and lead him step by step to
cope with the larger needs of his life.[1] Recall some of
the evidences of this Christian approach to teaching:

Jesus understood physical discomfort and suffering and seemed never to plunge in with a sermon
when people needed food or relief from pain.

Jesus understood the frustration of fear and acted
directly to remove the cause of fear--a storm at sea or
the mental disorder of a child.

Jesus understood the lonely and the unloved. His entire life was a display of genuine affection. "Return to your own house" was a command full of relief, for home is where one belongs and is loved.

Jesus understood the embarrassed and the outcast. Think of His psychological protection that shielded the adulterous woman from the scorn of the people, or of His dealings with the woman of Samaria. One is left feeling, not that He didn't care that these people had violated moral and social rules, but that he saw them as people of great worth. He seems to have sensed that at that moment they needed to have protection for their remaining self-respect (esteem) lest they should be completely destroyed.

Jesus understood a person's aspiration to be his very best and fullest self. Jesus summed up His mission in a single phrase--that all of us "may have life, and may have it in all its fullness."[2] He once talked to a man who wanted to live up to his potential. He told him that besides laying the proper moral foundation for his life, he should do the extravagant thing and be a philanthropist--give away his fortune and himself.

Jesus responded to the questions of those hungry to know and to understand. He explained ancient traditions, peeling away accumulated crusts and exposing the heart of moral and spiritual ideas behind empty practices. He patiently composed parables and similes to make the kingdom of heaven and the way of salvation fit inside the craniums of mere humans. He was always able to find an ordinary way of putting extraordinary truth.

Jesus was sensitive to our human need for beauty--for aesthetic satisfaction. There was a logic and harmony in His words and in His life that radiated and continues to radiate an uncommon beauty. He was intensely aware of all the beauty which He saw around Him.

It would be absurd to call this kind of personal interest human-centered education, because Jesus always managed to minister to the whole person in such a way as to lead him into a whole and fruitful relationship with God and with other people. What is clear, however, is that Jesus did not have a series of pat answers that He reduced to a set of sermons on how to be good. He did not try to talk people into living a new life through a series of lectures on how to be good. That is, the content of what He had to say was not Jesus' major concern. The person was His first concern--He came to minister to people. If you could know what a person's needs were, He seemed to believe, you could help him meet those needs and get on with the more important business of life.

If we want to be Christian in our church education, surely we can make a serious attempt to understand human needs. One study of human needs suggests that there is a ladder of needs common to all of us.[3] This ladder has seven ascending steps or kinds of needs. They are arranged in such a way that a person must meet lower level needs before he can sense the higher needs and cope with them. Here are some implications for us about those many splendored human needs:

Physical needs

Hunger, thirst, and pain are examples of physical needs. There are others. On our ladder of human needs they form the first rung. Most North Americans never experience severe hunger or thirst, but when one does, it is impossible for the typical person to give his attention to any other thing. Any alert teacher can detect the restlessness or the preoccupation of the student who is plagued by physical discomfort, exhaustion, or disease. It is not difficult at all to understand how our Lord was moved so often out of compassion for the sick and the hungry. Nor is it hard to discover where His pictures came from when He said, "When I was hungry you gave me nothing to eat, when thirsty nothing to drink."[4] The church--which cares for the whole person--must be alert to the physical needs of persons. James, the brother of our Lord, drives the arrow deep into our hearts when he says, "Suppose a brother or a sister is in rags with not enough food for the day, and one of you says, 'Good luck to you, keep yourselves warm, and have plenty to eat', but does nothing to supply their bodily needs, what is the good of that?"[5]

Security needs

The second step of the ladder of human needs has to do with security or safety needs. One who is in physical pain does not have the energy, time, or interest to consider the other threats to survival.

Indeed a desperate person may drink contaminated water or eat rancid food. But once the body is put at ease, the mind may turn to thoughts about safety.

All humans need an environment that is orderly, disciplined, and dependable; then they can give their attention to the higher needs. When a sense of threat hangs in the back of a child's mind, when an adult is facing the loss of an entire way of life, or when death deprives a family of a beloved member, no other ideas can compete for the attention that naturally is given to try to cope with the pressing crisis. "I'm sorry, I didn't hear what you said. Daddy left yesterday and said he isn't coming back." How could she possibly hear what we want to teach her? One can take the physical body to Sunday school, but if fear stalks the very existence or if jealousy (one specific form of fear) eats away at one's heart, very little can be learned until the monster is laid to rest.

Belongingness needs

The need for acceptance and love is the third rung that lies before the learner who has physical and safety needs met. All of us must come to believe that we are people of unique worth. We tend to judge our worth by the value placed on us by other people important in our lives. One would think that outside the home no other institution is more suited to lavishing affection and love upon individuals than the church. Indeed, many of us have formed our ideas about ourselves with the direct help of the fellowship of "those who care."

Two hazards exist, however, which may cause the Sunday school to stumble in meeting this need. (1) There is an inclination to close the circle of affection, unwittingly, including in it only those who have been in the circle for a long time. The newcomers--who may be reaching out in desperation for meaningful relationships--often have an uncomfortable sense that they have walked in on a private party, and they wait for a chance to break away and retreat to their already lonely problems. (2) We do not always accept people as they are when they come to us in the learning fellowship of the church. We violate the basic principle of Jesus' outgoing concern for all people in all conditions if we reject them by hostile glances or by our indifference. Unless we concentrate on meeting this need, which exists in everyone, we will likely fail Jesus here.

Status needs

Esteem or status needs stand as the fourth rung of our ladder. When physical, safety, and acceptance needs are met, we become aware of a yearning for evidence that we have earned our very own place. We need simple recognition.

The most important symbol to every person is his name. If I do not remember your name and you have been in my class on two consecutive Sundays, you have every reason to believe that you have not earned a significant place in my mind. If I want to give a real sense of success and earned status to the members of the class, I must match the abilities they have with important tasks that need to be done. When a person has been trusted to make a contribution through service, that person will feel a sense of worth among those being served.

Many churches systematically consult the congregational directory to be sure that every active member's name finds its way into the weekly newsletter. The annual birthday notice is the minimum mention. If the names are dated to indicate when the person has been named publicly, the coming opportunities are more likely to be directed to people who are consistently missing from the public eye.

Elective offices give status and thus express the esteem of others. So also do citations, awards, and invitations to participate as a discussion leader, host, or usher.

The need to be one's best self

All of the lower rungs of our ladder deal with the problems of how we see ourselves in relation to the outside world. When those relational needs have been met, we all yearn to entertain thoughts about becoming the people we are capable of becoming. "Who am I?" "What is my purpose in the world?" "What tasks need me?" These are questions that emerge as one becomes aware of "self-actualization" needs that cry out to be met.

It becomes evident that Sunday school teachers who aspire to teach their classes must consider whether their four fundamental physical and social needs are met. Then they can fully experience the joy of taking students on an exploration of "Who am I?" kinds of questions. At this point in our ladder of human needs, we see an opportunity to begin to minister to the deep needs of people. Indeed, only the message of the transforming grace of God through Jesus Christ offers anything like a complete blueprint for becoming a whole person.

Knowledge needs

The need to know and to understand elevates us to a yet higher rung of the ladder of human needs. There is a sense in which one might be motivated to learn by one's fear (the need for safety), by the desire to acquire status (the need for esteem), or even by the pursuit of becoming one's full self (the need for self-actualization). But there is increasing evidence that humans are equipped with a strong urge to explore and to understand.

Curiosity runs strong in the person who is free from the torment of the lower-level needs we have listed. We seem to be "attracted to the mysterious, to the unknown, to the chaotic, unorganized, and unexplained."[6] There are many people in the church who are curious. "Look at all of those people in there studying Genesis," a matronly newcomer said as she glanced into an adult Sunday evening class. "They've probably read it a hundred times in their lives, and they act as if it's brand new." She was quite unaware of the depth of the mine in which they were digging. Curiosity and the pursuit of the mysterious frequently lead us into intensive study.

Curiosity is especially evident in children and in young people. If it is curbed or discouraged, we tend to develop a generation of incurious and apathetic adults. "He stopped thinking thirty years ago" is an epitaph that should never be written for a Christian. "I couldn't possibly entertain the idea," a dear and admired author told me, "I am already 'in print' on the subject, so I can't change." I responded, "You are too young to die! Listen to Jesus and study Scripture. The most important part of your books is the date printed in the front. You are never too old to change and grow!"

If classes are drab or stifling to the curiosity, we fail the gift of God written into humans. We quench the flame of interest that sends them in search of answers.

Aesthetic needs

The need for beauty stands at the top of the ladder of human needs. Some people may never be conscious of this need at all. It is expressed by the demand for order (a sound argument), balance (a flower arrangement), symmetry (a pair of matched candles or horses), closure (a whole idea pieced together), and completion of the act (any job properly finished). While this need is considered last among human needs outlined here, and while the lower-scaled needs must be met before the aesthetic need becomes active, there is a sense in which it may appear as a part of other needs. For example, the need for knowledge leads some of us to organize a philosophy of life, to theorize about our own identity, and to develop a theological framework. As the thirst to know drives us deeper into philosophy and theology, there arises the demand that our conclusions take on an orderly, balanced shape. This demand for symmetry of ideas--call it "beauty"-- might be seen as a combination of intellectual and aesthetic needs.

Needs interlock and combine

Human needs are more complex than the "ladder of needs" suggests, just as any parable is simpler than what it represents. For example, a person in the same moment may be working to satisfy more than one need. Remember Jesus' runaway boy in the best-loved parable of all? In the monologue recorded in Luke 15, the young man exposes basic need for (1) satisfaction of physical distress--"I perish with hunger"; (2) longing for the safety of home; (3) longing for meaningful relationships with father and other persons-belongingness and love; and (4) the demand for better status--any way is *up* on the status ladder when you're imprisoned in a pigpen.

The human needs in our ladder represent the minimum needs of all humans of all ages. We know, for example, that all healthy children show aesthetic appreciation--a love of beauty. The infant also needs knowledge. Who would question that babies and also grandparents need esteem, or that all of us need to feel that we are accepted and that we are actively receiving and giving love?

Needs and teaching

Look at that class again. Outwardly they may appear poised. They may even seem to invite you to bombard them with information for 40 minutes. The apparent readiness to listen may be only a well-practiced courtesy.

How can you know what the real needs of individuals are? What can you do to help them become whole people--their own best selves? Is more information their first and greatest need?

We must explore some possible ways for sharing information and ideas. But first we must probe further to find ways to help bring persons to wholeness, "teaching everyone in all wisdom; that we may present every person complete in Christ Jesus."[7]

3
People, Wholeness, and Holiness

In a series of radio plays written for the BBC and entitled The Man Born to Be King, Dorothy Sayers has Mary Magdalene in conversation with her brother and with Jesus. Mary, whose reputation as a sinner was widely known, thinks about her reckless past and says to her brother, "You tried to tame my wild spirits. If I had listened to you I should never have sinned so deeply. But there was so much--so much to enjoy. I loved the beauty of the world. I loved the lights and the laughter, the jewels and the perfumes and the gold, and the applause of the people when I danced and delighted them all, with garlands of lilies in the red braids of my hair."

Her brother responds: "You are always in love with life."

"I love the wrong things in the wrong way--yet it was love of a sort . . . until I found a better."

Jesus interrupts her: "Because the love was so great, the sin is all forgiven."

To this reminder of her transformation, Mary recalls her thoughts on the night when she first met Jesus: "You told me so, when I fell at your feet in the house of Simon the Pharisee. . . . Did you know? My *companions and I came there that day to mock you. We thought you would be sour and grim, hating all beauty and treating life as an enemy. But when I saw you, I was amazed. You were the only person there that was really alive. The rest of us were going about half-dead--making the gestures of life, pretending to be real people. The life was not with us but with you-- intense and shining, like the strong sun when it rises and turns the flames of our candles to pale smoke. And I wept and was ashamed, seeing myself such a thing of trash and tawdry. But when you spoke to me, I felt the flame of the sun in my heart. I came alive for the first time. And I love life all the more since I have its meaning."*

Sayers has Jesus answer with words found essentially in John 10:10. "That is what I am here for. I came that men should lay hold of life and possess it to the full."[1]

The Christian task and a caution

If the church does the work of Jesus, it is clear that people should be called from brokenness to wholeness and from emptiness to fullness when the claims of God are laid upon their lives. If the church stoops instead to fulfill the ambitions of self-centered members, it is conceivable that folks will be called, not to wholeness and freedom, but to lives that are warped and enslaved. Jesus had words of stern warning for those who go out to win converts just to cast them into their own mold: "You travel over sea and land to win one convert; and when you have won him you make him twice as fit for hell as you are yourselves."[2]

Jesus' charge seems to suggest that if you impose a religion of mere external rules for behavior upon pagans--make that person like yourself--you cut off the possibility that such people will ever find how to become their own best selves. You have also started such people off in a way of thinking that warps their entire way of looking at themselves and at God and has them doing the right things for the wrong reasons. Such people are thus twice as lost as their "evangelists," who may in some sincere moment discover or go in search of the roots of faith from which their rigid set of rules have sprung.

Created for wholeness

Diversity is written into the whole universe, but nowhere more strikingly than in humans. We were created to blossom into independence and to manage and order our world--to "have dominion." Not only were we to be fully responsible for the creative management of the world but we were created for a life-long adventure--striving to become the kind of people God has created us to become.

The Genesis account pictures the first human as whole and complete. Our human sense of who we are was rooted in the original human's intimate relationship with God--relationship in which the human was at once dependent and self-directing. The "Adam" enjoyed both dominion and freedom. Once "split" into female and male, they lived by the strength of meaningful relationships between male and female in the original community--a microcosm which remains the reminder of our human need for significance and intimate sharing. That trust was symbolized by nakedness, which gave way to the secrecy of a clothed society.[3]

The ultimate tragedy of the human race shattered both our human intimacy with God and our trust in each other. The woman, literally *Ishah* found all of her relationships damaged, including the prospect of being separated by profound pain from the children she would bear. The man, literally *Ish,* was compulsively drawn to labor and "things," even reducing his *Ishah* to a new and demeaning name--his property, "Eve, the one who makes babies." Instead of absolute mutual respect between himself and the "bone of my bone and flesh of my flesh" *Ishah, Ish* would find her estranged from him, driven by the desire to be his adversary. But his impulses would run toward "lording it over her."

Humans everywhere have, ever since, been in search of personal identity--to find out who we are. This search is often pursued in intense and dangerous ways. Yet we all behave as we do because of the way we see our unique situations and the courses of action we see open to us. If we can accept this as a working principle to explain individual behavior, then in the educational work of the church we will accept everyone *as they are.* If we truly accept people, we do far more than merely tolerate them. We try to see things from their point of view and to understand what courses of action they see open. We try to understand the concepts they have of themselves and the future they see for themselves. Then we will interpret their present behavior as a sincere effort to achieve their goals for themselves within the limitation of the options they see available.

If we work for this understanding of people, there are, then, two grand opportunities open to us: (1) We can help folks enlarge and enrich their pictures of what they may become. This enlargement of vision will allow them to change their actions in pursuit of higher goals for themselves. (2) We can offer additional ways to achieve their goals effectively.

Out of all of our human needs, then, we have found the one which finally drives us all our lives. Our consistent consuming need is "to be that self which one truly is,"[4] or, in the words of our Lord, to possess life "in all its fullness."[5]

Helping people to wholeness

Try, now, to apply our working principle to people you know well. Imagine that instead of lashing out at someone or judging them on the spot, you say, "That person is behaving that way because of some desperate inner need. What is that need? How does my friend see himself and his need? By what reasoning is this particular action chosen to help achieve the goal in mind?"

Perhaps no one is better able to ask these kinds of

questions than those who are transformed and growing Christians. These people are well on their way to productive and radiant Christian living. They have discovered who they are, and they have found the basic source of satisfaction for the gnawing needs of their lives. No doubt you have been given responsibility in the educational work of the church because you are a responsible and growing Christian. Here are some guidelines that may help you to help other people to wholeness:

1. *Care for people as they are.* People who have found themselves through Christian renewal tend to want to help other folks find themselves. It is important to remember that Jesus accepted us as we were; His probing was at a deeper level than that of the visible or social. He made us restless about our emptiness and our purposelessness and our estrangement from His Father.

If you really care about individuals in your class, you will be intent upon knowing them well. You will talk to them about things that interest *them*. Listen in on your next conversation to see how much of the time the conversation centers around your own interests; why do you *need* to talk so much about *you*--what *you* have done, seen, known, or felt? People who care have a way of turning a conversation to bring out the other person's point of view and interests. Then, learn to listen. Listen not only for a person's words, but for what the deeper message is *really* trying to tell you. It may be something quite different from the words you hear.

If you really care about people, you will encourage

and support them. You will call attention to their strong points and play down their weaknesses. Jesus never embarrassed a needy person by focusing on past failure or present weaknesses.

If you care deeply, you will cultivate independence of thought and action in other people. The Christian who thinks and makes decisions for other people has not helped them to wholeness; instead the other folks have only become more crippled by dependency. We will have made "proselytes" who are in danger of being lost because they were twisted instead of transformed.

2. *Cultivate honesty and openness.* If you have faced the truth about yourself and laid yourself open to God, you can be honest with other people. If you are a false face, your students will keep their masks on, too. Have you never disappointed yourself or Jesus? Have you never struggled with doubts? Or walked through the valley of the shadow? Have you never thought a heretical thought? Admit it. Within the learning fellowship of the church one ought to be able to find the freest and warmest atmosphere in the world. Here we should be able to accept ourselves and other people and their viewpoints. We can do this in the church because the Lord of the church is the Lord of truth, and the Lord of the church is the Lord of freedom. He and all of His transformed people are surely confident and poised enough to let stumbling, groping persons voice their fears, their doubts, their disbeliefs, and their hopes. Honesty is the only foundation on which you can cultivate a learning fellowship that enjoys an atmosphere of freedom and invites an open exchange

of ideas and attitudes.

3. *Begin where people are.* Remember that there can be no learning unless needs are met. Think of the kinds of needs the individuals in your class are wrestling with: (a) Personal needs arising from their own private experience. These will differ with each individual; many of those needs cannot be handled directly in class discussion. But you may be able to arrange the learning experiences in such a way as to minister to those needs, perhaps coming in sideways to meet them. (b) Needs arising in the common experiences of the class. Suppose that an untimely death has left your class in shock. Death is a great mystery; most of us need to discuss and develop a healthy Christian view of it. Take advantage of the need to understand death and draw students into what might be one of the most meaningful discussions of their lifetimes. (c) Undefined needs that can be awakened or brought to the surface will often set the stage for bringing needs into focus. You can work with role playing or use a dramatic reading of a problem-filled dialogue to help students identify their own problems and needs.

These kinds of needs--personal, group, and undefined needs--offer you an opportunity to intersect the real lives of your students. You can arrange the learning experiences in such a way that what they need to know can be made to collide with those things that are troubling them. Remember that Jesus began within the experiences and needs of the woman of Samaria.[6] He then introduced an element of curiosity by speaking of "living water." He accepted her invitation to a brief debate about where one should worship. Notice, too, that Jesus heard beyond her words what she was really saying. One has the distinct impression that the woman's interests and real needs are skillfully brought together--made to intersect--by our Lord. We easily call Him the Master Teacher.

"New folks, re-created in holiness"[7]

We observed that humans were created for wholeness--for meaningful relationships with God and with other people. We have also taken as a working principle for ourselves the fact that all of us make choices based on the way we see our situation and the courses of action open to us.

Within the warmth of the learning fellowship of the church, people should be able to find ways to expand their vision of their possible selves. At the same time they will likely discover the effective steps to take in order to achieve those supreme goals. The learning fellowship of the church, then, may well serve as the midwife at the new birth of people who enter into the kingdom of our Lord. But this can occur only if needs are met; indeed, only if they are deliberately studied and served. No number of classes or superficial measures of religious knowledge can assure spiritual birth to a learner.

The person who is converted or renewed is restored, set back into the original pattern for which we were created. Indeed, the transformation is better than the original naive innocence. We are now re-created in knowledge, in righteousness, and in true holiness.[8] All of this is made possible by the reconciliation of Jesus Christ. The renewed person is "conformed to the image of [God's] Son."[9]

When we have found that reconciliation with God and other people, we have been restored to holiness. The old theologians have long spoken of "initial holiness" as well as of "entire" or "inward holiness," which comes only with the deep inward cleansing of human affections and motivations by God's Spirit. Wholeness, then, has its effect at the very core of our existence. The person who finds wholeness has, when it is most simply put, found holiness in the quality of all his relationships. John Wesley noted that God's grace produces both real and relative changes in us. We are really made righteous; we do not simply have an appearance or a covering under which the same old unrighteous self remains. And all relationships are changed--relationships with God, with other people, and with the created world.

Marks of the whole person: A checklist

☐ The whole person takes a generally positive view of the self.[10] We should turn out to be the world's greatest realists. We can face the truth about ourselves. Our repentance was the most courageous act of our lives. We are saints in the making, and we know both our weaknesses and our strengths. Jesus implied self-respect when He admonished us to love our neighbors

51

as ourselves.[11] The Apostle Paul, out of abundant experiences of frustration, wrote: "I have the strength to face all conditions by the power that Christ gives me."[12]

☐ The whole person is able to cope with all kinds of experiences that come along. Because of our essentially positive attitudes we are not shattered by opposition or by the threats of others.[13] Jesus, from the cross, retained His poise and His concern for other persons. He dispatched instructions for the care of His mother. He comforted a terrified but penitent criminal. And He urged forgiveness for the execution squad. Paul gives a graphic description of the whole person's extraordinary poise: "We are no better than pots of earthenware to contain this treasure, and this proves that such transcendent power does not come from us, but is God's alone. Hard-pressed on every side, we are never hemmed in; bewildered, we are never at our wits' end; hunted, we are never abandoned to our fate; struck down, we are not left to die."[14]

☐ The whole person can feel strongly the needs of other people. We do not have to struggle to think of others; our concern for them is the by-product of the basic reorganization of our own lives. We find ourselves feeling the suffering of other folks, seeing things from their points of view, and acting out of compassion to give of ourselves to meet their needs. Of these "new" people, C.S. Lewis wrote: "They do not draw attention to themselves. You tend to think that you are being kind to them when they are really being kind to you. They love you more than other [folks] do, but they need you less. . . . They will usually seem to have a lot of time: you will wonder where it comes from."[15]

☐ The whole person tends to be creative and spontaneous. Having made peace in all of our relationships and having acquired a poised honesty and realism, our energies are released from self-defense and making masks. Our energy goes into nobler purposes. We can turn to creative and useful activities with a relaxed spontaneity as the "image of God" is being restored and completed in us.[16]

☐ The whole person is not a slave to conformity. Such people are the backbone of the human race and keep their bearings when mass insanity is the mode of the day. They possess a dignity and integrity which is rooted within their transformed view of themselves in their new relationships. The Apostle Paul described the need for this kind of independence: "Don't let the world around you squeeze you into its own mold, but let God remold your minds from within."[17]

Meeting needs with information and ideas

We have explored the fundamental needs of people and found that teaching must take those needs into account not only because they threaten to hinder teaching but also because they are cues that often tell us what it is that folks are most ready to learn. It is important that we turn next to examine how we deal with facts and ideas in meaningful ways in the act of learning.

4

Can I Teach
a Million Facts?

*Do you remember the anecdote about a man who
requested a preaching license from his church board?
They, in turn, asked for an interview and the opportunity to ask questions:*

"What is your favorite book of the Bible?"

"Why, the book of Parables," he answered.

*"Tell us something of what is in that book," they
asked.*

*"Well," said the aspiring young preacher, "a certain
man went down from Jerusalem to Jericho, and he fell
among thieves. May the thorns grow up and choke the
thieves. After they had robbed him he went on his way
until he came to Jericho, and there sitting high up on
the wall he saw Jezebel. And he heard the men shout-
ing, 'Throw her down.' Then, they said, 'Throw her
down again.' Finally a voice cried and said, 'How
many times shall I throw her down?' And they said,
'Throw her down seventy times seventy times.' And of
the fragments they picked up twelve baskets full. Now,
whose wife do you think she will be in the judgment?"*

The complexity of facts to learn

The whole thing must have been fiction, and the response of the church board is conveniently not known. The anecdote does serve to remind us of how complex Bible facts are and of the vast quantity of material to be learned. The Bible is a whole library of books written by more than three dozen authors. Its recorded events cover more than four thousand years. It is largely the account of people bearing strange names. They lived in lands not easy to associate with present countries. Some names appear many times but refer to different people. The Bible is not arranged entirely in chronological order; indeed, some books coming from the same period of time are widely separated in their locations in the Bible. In some cases, several books cover the same events from various points of view, as in the case of the Gospels.

To further complicate matters, the Bible contains a variety of kinds of literature--historical narrative, epic poetry, family trees, hymns, parables, sermons, and predictive prophecy. Each kind of literature must be read for what it is and not as if it were another class of literature.

If mastery of only the purely factual material in the Bible were our goal, a lifetime of serious study would likely fall short of achieving it. Yet the traditional approach to Bible study in the Sunday school takes us repeatedly to the same events or stories. This tends to frustrate the growing children, who imagine that we are wanting them to learn "facts." It is equally frustrating to the teacher who grows weary with repeated handling of elementary information. Besides Bible material, we expect everybody in the church to master certain other kinds of facts. They study Christian beliefs, sometimes from a church catechism. They study church history and church organization. They study the art of Christian living and of being good church members.

The problem of remembering

The human mind is capable of storing enormous quantities of information. A few people are evidently able to store an entire book almost in perfect detail. Many readers can recall not only what they have read but also the precise location on the page where the words may be found again. Yet, nearly all of us remember only a fraction of what we have read.

There may not be a great deal of comfort in the fact, but we are told that our problem is not one of memory; it is one of retrieval. That is, we remember an immense quantity of information, but it is stored in our heads in such a way that we cannot locate it for use when we need it. Research on the human ability to remember gives us a picture of how fast we lose the sharp details we have learned. The high point in this graph represents twenty minutes after one has mastered a series of nonsense words. Notice how fast memory shrinks during the first few hours. Finally, the line levels off at a modest plane showing how many of the learned sounds can be recalled up to thirty-one days later. This line can be lifted by re-

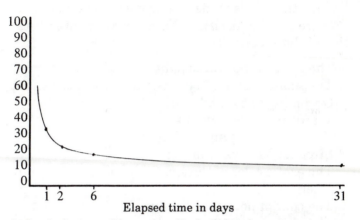

A classical curve of forgetting. Early Ebbinghaus experiments, 1885.[1]

peated review. But the line can be lifted greatly if the material is also meaningful. A college professor who travels the same specialized track year after year, for example, builds up an impressive level of factual recall. But this is not to say that he or she can display the same competence with other facts that are processed through the mind day by day.

Perception: ground floor of learning

Perception[2] refers simply to the conscious recognition of what is going on about us. Perception occurs at a very rapid rate. The typical person processes several million perceptions each day. When you are driving the automobile through city traffic, you are receiving literally thousands of cues through your several senses. You are making decisions based on your interpretation of those perceptions:

The color of the traffic light
The sudden lurch of a pedestrian toward the street
Oncoming autos and trucks
Traffic to the left and to the right
Your own fuel gauge or high beam signal
Street or highway markers
The exotic color of the sports car passing on your left
The odor of hot brake linings
The air temperature and the comfort of your passengers
The sound of a manhole cover as you pass over it
A flashing light and ambulance siren
The diesel odor of a city bus

You move through this sea of facts with no thought of ever wanting to recall the perceptions you made as you passed through. Yet your mind was carefully sorting out information and making decisions to move you home safely.

When we suggest that perception is the ground floor for learning in the classroom, we are only saying that learners bring their minds to the session, and their thinking operates there most of the time simply at the data-processing level. That is, they process the sights and sounds about them, examine them for their familiarity, and make the decisions the facts demand of them. What troubles us is that two hours later, at Sunday dinner, Johnny or Jenny may have very little to share from their class experiences. They may have no more to share, in fact, than you did Friday evening when your spouse asked you at dinner, "Did anything interesting happen on your way home from work?" And you paused a moment and said, "Not that I recall, but I *did* see a chartreuse MG roadster at the corner of Broadway and Main."

The public school has traditionally had ways of motivating Johnny or Jenny to remember the *percepts* they processed while passing through English I. They have been told that they must remember many of their perceptions because week-by-week samples will be taken on a test to see whether they are learning. What is more, there is a day of reckoning coming at the end of the term, and a final exam at the end of the semester. Johnny and Jenny will then be responsible for everything they have processed through their craniums during the entire course. It is up to the children to find ways of retrieving this information from the storage equipment in their minds.

Johnny and Jenny have several courses of action they may take: (1) They may develop a private system of filing grammatical rules, principles of word usage, and accurate spelling for rapid recall. (2) They may review daily or weekly, keeping in mind what they have learned so as to have it all ready for the day of judgment. (3) They may check out the logic and integrity of each percept, accept but not try to retain those which ring true, and hold the difficult percepts for further digestion, releasing them from consciousness when they fit the logic of the system. In doing this they are probably saying that how well they do on the test is not very important; they are more interested in seeing that English makes sense to them as they meet it. (4) They may carry their books to class, listen sometimes, and take their chances on the tests.

The educational ministry of the church has rarely used tests to motivate students to remember what they have learned. Certain memorization requirements must be met for awards or even for membership training, but these stand outside the major educational program of the church. At best we have hoped that Johnny and Jenny are using their minds according to plan number 3, above, but we have suspected that many of our students follow plan number 4.

The number 3 option, however, has considerable merit. Follow-up research now seems to be showing that once our youngsters are out of school, those who worked hard to learn whether things rang true in their understanding move quickly ahead of their classmates who studied to match wits with the teacher. The difference evidently is one of meaningfulness. What comes alive in your mind because it takes on meaning evidently lives longer than what you file by some artificial system for short-range recall to pass a test.

Organizing facts meaningfully

Experiments with adults and their ability to recall meaningless information show that their ability is limited to the recall of what has been called "the magical number seven, plus or minus two."[3] Whether you can name the twelve apostles, or only seven, is probably related to whether their names are meaningful to you. Where do you look in your mental equipment to find them filed? Under "Authors of New Testament books"? Under "Principal people in the public ministry of Jesus"? Or under "History of missionary activities and church growth"? You probably have no "Names of Apostles" category unless you acquired it in some memorization program. How many can you name?[4] Now subtract those you had filed "meaningfully."

Meaningful learning seems to occur only when facts are woven into a meaningful fabric of related information, and the fabric or structure is most meaningful if it is developed by the learner.[5] A "fact" in isolation is almost certainly doomed to extinction, but if it can be filed with related material, it stands a fair chance for survival as a distinct fact. What may be more important--indeed what we will examine a little later--is that it may contribute to the formation of a larger idea. As a part of the larger idea it may lose its distinct identity. You may not be able to recall it in the form in which it was filed, but it has contributed to building an important and permanent part of your mental equipment.

For the moment, imagine that all facts come packaged in single units, each of which fit into a cell of a honeycomb. Now, imagine that you give each single fact a slight magnetic charge that tells the category in which to find related information already in the honeycomb. Piece by piece the facts begin to form an organized colony within the framework provided for them.[6] They occasionally shift to make room for new information that fills in the logic or the missing pieces of larger ideas or concepts. We now know that if you "file away" factual material that is charged with some emotion, it will be highlighted for longer and more efficient retrieval--it will be "imprinted" through that special emotion.

Teaching for meaning

It becomes very important, then, that learning experiences in the church furnish people information which they can organize meaningfully for permanent use. Fortunately, Christian education is carried out with conceptual material and is done in a special environment where the emotional tone may make the learning particularly easy to recall. Here are some guidelines for all of us who have anything to do with teaching. If we follow them, we are well on the way to increasing the meaningfulness of learning in the church.

1. Acquire a careful understanding of the structures or concepts that we need to know. The learner who is confused in perception is frequently confused because basic information has been omitted or carelessly handled. The teacher must be willing to crawl inside the developing mind of students and to imagine what basic cells remain empty in the mental honeycomb. It is a special privilege to highlight specific cells of memory because the learning took place in a warm

caring environment.

2. Discover ways to break into the consciousness of passive students to bring their present needs into intersection with information that they can build into life-changing ideas.

3. Arouse curiosity for information that is useful in building big ideas. Sharing in fresh discovery with students, is an exciting adventure that will enrich even the well-trained teacher in the church.

4. Offer temporary ways of organizing information for meaning. Your students must finally develop their own systems, but give a temporary magnetic charge to important facts and show how a cluster of facts is beginning to form a concept.

5. Share the excitement of discovery. In the Christian fellowship we are all frontline research scholars, making our own discoveries, organizing our own observations, and constantly sharing the good news of our findings with new recruits.

What will they remember?

Several dozen "percepts" may eventually cluster into a single "concept" ("con" = with). Some of the percepts will retain their identities in the mind of the learner. These bits of information that stand out within a concept are remembered. For example, in the concept "sanctification" one might recall the fact "disciples of our Lord are sanctified through the truth; God's word is truth." One might even recall that this fact is stated in John 17:17.

How are concepts formed? What keeps the clusters together? And what holds the identity of percepts within a concept? These are questions which are crucial for us, since meaningful learning in the church must build for the big ideas.

Before we explore the construction of concepts, however, we must ask whether there are facts which should be learned for their own sake. If so, how will they be held in memory? What is the place of memorization in meaningful learning in the church?

5

To Memorize or Not

More than five hundred people applauded as four teenagers walked into the spotlight. The master of ceremonies had just announced them: "Ladies and Gentlemen, it is my pleasure to present the International Bible Quiz Championship Team."

The team--three regular members and one substitute--had climbed from obscurity in the hills of eastern Kentucky to win conference and international tournaments by combining jumping speed with factual accuracy in answering perhaps a total of a thousand competition questions drawn from the Book of Acts.

Standing there in the spotlight receiving trophies, gold-imprinted Bibles, and one-thousand-dollar scholarships to the denominational liberal arts college of each team member's choice, they represented more than one hundred other quizzers who had made it to the international tournament. These, in turn, represented an estimated one thousand contestants whose teams lost out in conference competition, some of them by very narrow margins. Those many teams were formed out of local Bible study groups often three or four times the size of the final team admitted to the conference and international competition.

Among quizzers it is common for members to have memorized, letter perfect, whole blocks of chapters of the book on which they are competing. Within the team personnel an entire book is sometimes held in memory; an occasional quizzer is said to have memorized an entire book.

All of this took place, not in 1900, when everybody in the church drilled on Scripture memorization, but in 1967, at a time when few people were taking pains to memorize very much. "Bible Quizzing" remains a popular teen competition today.

Primitive cultures and memorization

Cultures in which books and other written records are scarce rely almost exclusively upon memorization to preserve their heritage. In such a culture the really important information is usually woven into rituals, poems, or songs. These spoken forms have a powerful survival ability. The ritual survives by its regular repetition according to a specific pattern. The poem and the song survive because they are incorporated into the social life of the culture and thus enjoy frequent repetition. They are particularly suited for survival without change because rhyme and meter hold them together and tend to freeze the words (and thus the facts) into an unchanging form. Oral tradition has an outstanding record of holding content with very little change across many generations.

At the beginning of this century there was a scarcity of books, but now there is an explosion of printed materials. During this period of transition we have seen a corresponding decline in emphasis upon memorization. It is possible that there is a relationship between our immersion in literature and our loss of interest in memorization.

Memorization in a technological age

Modern westerners are producing more literature than any one person could consume; we are actively involved in more interpersonal and international political events than we can possibly understand. Besides, we are part of a generation that has unleashed a mushrooming fund of technical and scientific knowledge. Typically, we have chosen to learn a great deal about some small, narrowly defined segment of our culture. We then work as a relatively unknown member of a large team of highly specialized professionals and make our contribution toward the further push for knowledge and toward applying the benefits of existing knowledge to the present culture. One has the feeling that some major catastrophe could paralyze our technological culture and throw us back into a hewing and carving stone-age existence. If scarce knowledge existed only in the minds of skilled people and had never been committed to written form, we could be only one heartbeat from a new stone age.

When you visit ancient Aztec or Egyptian ruins, you glimpse evidences of an advanced culture. It is almost inevitable that you will be awed by the accomplishments of ancient people. Theirs was an age, however, in which the marvelous secrets of construction, medicine, and science were the private property of a few people of keen insight or unusual luck. The only way to preserve a secret was to keep it in one's head--to memorize it. Fathers or mothers, for example, could pass on the secrets to their children, who in turn could memorize them. But if disease or conquest wiped out the wizards who possessed this scarce intelligence, the culture threw back to the dark night of ignorance. Information and skills could be forever lost.

The rapid advance of European and North American culture is credited largely to lifting the secrecy from scarce knowledge. The practice of consultation among doctors of medicine and the keeping of records broke open private secrets and began the accumulation of a fund of medical knowledge. The price you paid for laying your secrets open before your fellow professionals was the loss of status as a mystical miracle worker, but the payoff more than offset the loss of private secrets as knowledge began its slow but sure explosion.

Today's culture is essentially an open-knowledge culture. To store our knowledge, we have founded ever-expanding libraries. We have developed microfilming techniques to reduce the problem of storing scarce and voluminous data. We have now witnessed the first of what will surely be a long series of rapid-retrieval, copying, and transmitting processes. Today, information stored in some remote library may be conveyed photographically by telephone and communications satellite virtually anywhere in the world. You may even install a fax machine for transmitting printed material using a telephone line.

In an open-knowledge culture it is less important to have a large fund of scarce knowledge filed in one's head than it is to know where to turn for the specific bit of knowledge you need in one of your many complex tasks. The physicist, for example, does not attempt to remember the intricate details of an experiment which has been carried out over a period of a dozen weeks. Instead, the scientist carefully reduces the findings not only to a formula that can be shared with others who may want to repeat the experiment, but also to a formula so compact that anyone can carry it around in his head--can memorize it. Except for occasional memorizing for convenience or for fun, we tend to limit our memorization to this expandable kind of formula, which can be useful in many settings with a variety of circumstances.

Christian education and memorization

The Christian community has witnessed a similar mushrooming of knowledge. Religious, devotional, and serious theological writings and observations are being published at an unprecedented rate. Whereas once the serious Christian might have been expected to memorize not only Bible passages but also passages from Milton, Augustine, and Jerome, today's serious disciple is more likely to spend learning time moving through the body of religious literature in a rapid process more for enrichment than for memorization.

Today's Christian might have memorized these kinds of materials:

Selected Bible passages
The Apostles' Creed
The catechism
Names of the books of the Bible
A few dozen hymns (accidentally memorized)

The guideline which applies in a technological culture at large also might be applied in church education: Memorize "formula value" material that will be useful to you under a variety of circumstances and that can be transformed and expanded for continuing useful application. Curriculum planners, teachers, and parents are confronted with deciding what to include in the memorization program for children and young people, and for themselves.

Repetition

Memorization cannot occur unless there are opportunities for the learner to repeat the material dozens or even hundreds of times. A teacher must decide whether a particular memorization task is of sufficient importance to invest scarce class time to the repetition, either by group recitation or by the individual students. If class time is not available, the teacher can arrange presession practice time or attempt to arrange for repetition practice at home.

As we become increasingly aware of the importance of developing concepts, we tend to decrease the stress on rote memorization in the class session. Indeed, Sunday school in most churches seventy-five years ago was almost entirely carried out by following a rote system of questions, responses, and repetition. Here is an example of recommended Sunday school procedure in 1919:

Supt.--What is the Golden Text?
School.--Seek ye first the kingdom of God, and his righteousness. Matt. 6:33.
Practical Truth.--**Nothing can be as good for us as a believer's part in the kingdom of God.**
Topic.--**The universality of the kingdom.**
Time.--**Parables spoken, A.D. 28.**
Place.--**Capernaum.**[2]

This formal block appeared each week, printed, conveniently, in lightface and boldface type to indicate which part the "Superintendent" read and which part was for the "School" to read. Besides, the Scripture was printed in alternating type-faces and was clearly labeled: "Supt." and "School."

The rigid format has given way to a freer exploration of Christian truth and ideas. It seems that the more our resources and our fund of information increases, the more free we are to explore the rich ideas and experiences awaiting our investigation. Rote forms and memorization have largely been left to private or household hours, where repetition time can be better justified than it is in the classroom. There, discussion, inquiry, and exploration are more pressing obligations.

Chaining

A second ingredient that must be present for effective memorization is sometimes called "chaining." Chaining refers to linking together two sounds or events in such a way that when the first is produced it calls forth the second in immediate succession. Most of us find, for example, that when we are memorizing anything, we can do it more quickly if we work aloud. The sounds then take on more power to stimulate succeeding sounds in the chain. Finally, of course, we are able to run the chain through our minds in silence and to experience the firing of one link after another.

If you have memorized the books of the Bible, you probably did so as a child before the names of the books had any significant meaning to you. The names may have been meaningless sounds to you then. You no doubt astounded your elders, however, with your facility in spilling them at a moment's notice. Even now, as then, if you lose your chain, say, at *Esther,* the chances are good that you will have to go back to the beginning to set off the firing pattern all over: Genesis-Exodus- Leviticus-Numbers, and so forth. It may take several re-firings to get *Esther* to trigger *Job* and move you on toward the end of the list.

Chaining is helped if you can add additional tracks.

For example, a poetic version of the material would add the track of meter and perhaps rhyme as well. If you can put the material to music, you have added the track of melody (or harmony if you are singing a voice part in a group). Your chances of recall are greater, and retention will be longer, if you have more than the single firing of sound patterns. You develop what amounts to simultaneous firings on each of the tracks as you combine elements of sound, meter, rhythm, and melody.

Perhaps you memorized the names of books of the New Testament as set to a simple tune with a few intervening phrases to achieve rhyme. If so, you probably find yourself almost unconsciously running through the pattern in your mind--would you dare to hum under your breath!--when the pastor announces a reading from Philemon.

In the American history information survey reported in chapter 1, eight of the nine respondents gave the answer "Paul Revere" for the question "Who was the American patriot who rode into Concord to warn the villagers that the British were coming?" This was one item which could be answered from one's "memory file." Many of us learned Longfellow's "Listen, my children, and you shall hear/Of the midnight ride of Paul Revere." The metrical, rhyming track held the name perfectly in memory. It is regrettable that Longfellow was less attentive to the facts than to his rhyming scheme, however, since the first patriot messenger to reach Lexington and Concord was a man named Samuel Prescott. Revere was captured, and even his companion, Dawes, encountered difficulty but finally arrived at Concord on foot only to find that the news had preceded him.

External reward

Psychologists remind us that memorization is achieved with maximum efficiency only when there is some external reward given to the learner:

The praise of someone important in one's life
The approval or applause of friends of one's own age
A letter grade in school
Entering the accomplishment in some permanent record
Certificate of award
Trophy
Photograph in the newspaper
Prizes

Remember the Nikita Khrushchev incident in which he is reported to have memorized all of the Four Gospels for candy prizes?

This kind of reward has a great appeal to many children and young people, and the size or significance of the reward needs to be appropriate to the age and interest of the person. Young children do not need a gold-plated trophy, for example, to motivate them to learn the names of the books of the Old Testament or the Ten Commandments. The Bible quizzer who is seventeen years old, however, has about exhausted the available external rewards, as the accumulated list of them suggests: trophy, imprinted Bible, one-thousand-dollar scholarship, and the super-reward of wild applause and awesome attention given by those all-important peers at a national convention.

Adults who choose to memorize tend to do so for their own reasons--not for external reward. They frequently complain that they "just can't do it" as they once could. And they are right. The difficulty probably comes from the lack of time for repetition combined with the absence of any inclination to respond to a set of rewards that they might set up: No dessert tonight unless I know John 14 word for word. One dollar set aside for missions each day until I know the chapter perfectly. But these seem inappropriate to many adults, and memorization is looked upon as a kind of magical ability that God gives to children but takes from adults.

The future of memorization

It is likely that in the church we will continue to find many "formula" quality bodies of information that should be committed to memory for permanent use. High on the list will be a variety of Bible passages that are useful in sustaining the courage and commitment of one's own faith. There are other passages we should know if we want to share our faith with other people.

No doubt we will continue to feel that some sets of information--names of Bible books, catechism, the Ten Commandments, the Lord's Prayer, for example--

need to be memorized even before the words are meaningful. Perhaps there are other blocks of information that would continue to enrich and to serve throughout adult life. If so, these should be set up for memorization during the years when memorization time and motivation potential are at their peaks.

Nevertheless, in the classroom with its limited time, we must devote our energies more often to helping our young and ourselves find the deep meaning of our faith. And that meaning is rarely guaranteed by memorization.

6

Acquiring the Really Big Ideas

"Of course, Noah was a Christian!"

"No, he wasn't," someone disagreed; "he couldn't have been. Jesus hadn't even been born when Noah lived."

"Well, all right. But if he had lived when Jesus did, he would have been a Christian."

A class of fourth, fifth, and sixth grade children at Sunday school were making up a rule to define "Christian." At first the class was unanimous in declaring that Noah was a Christian. The decision was written on the chalkboard where five other Bible persons were being classified. When they finally got Saul of Tarsus transformed into Paul the apostle, they had discovered a requirement which put personal response to Jesus Christ at the very heart of the definition. So, that threw out Noah.

When the definition met the approval of everyone in the class, the teacher offered still another problem.

"Now, I have a very difficult question for you." He hesitated. "In fact, it may be too hard for you to try to answer." They insisted that he state it.

"All right. Was Jesus a Christian?"

There was silence -- absolute silence for several sec-

onds. The children were not startled; they only needed time to turn to their definition to tell whether Jesus was a Christian or to see whether they needed to define it still further. Finally one of the boys responded confidently.

"No. Jesus was God; He didn't need a Savior. He didn't have any sin."

The children were expanding their concepts and forming working principles to guide them throughout life. This teaching-learning strategy is particularly useful to the parent, to the teacher, or to any adult who is concerned that children and young people learn more than facts."

Clustering facts into concepts

Imagine that the many facts we acquire are filler for a kind of mental honeycomb. Then imagine that we store those facts in compartments clustered according to the various ideas that are taking shape in our heads. These clusters of facts are the first shape of concepts as they begin to build.[1]

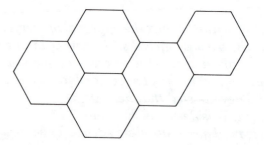

I mentioned earlier that there are five major concepts that give one's Christian faith its distinctive shape. These were concepts of God, humanity, sin, salvation, and the world.[2] These five guiding concepts tend to form in an interlocking way. One's particular conception of God, for example, interlocks with a specific view of humanity, for we live in relationship to God, and the two concepts must be harmonious. So also, one's view of God and of ourselves interlocks with ideas about sin and salvation, for these two concepts are rooted in an understanding of the way we are estranged from God, how serious that estrangement is, and what must be done to repair the vital relationship between the human race and God.

You could picture the five concepts as five fragments of a honeycomb, related in such a way that some of the smaller facts or percepts extend from one concept through all of the remaining four.

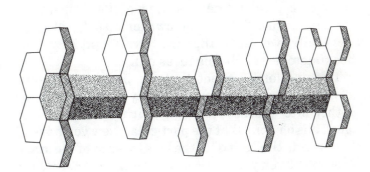

Here are some of the percepts that might be found clustering in these five concepts. Notice the interlocking aspects of some percepts:

God	Humanity	Sin	Salvation	World
Creator	The created	Estrange-ment	Reconcili-ation	The creation
Holiness	Potential holiness	Unholiness	Holiness restored	"good"
Fellowship with man	Fellowship with God	Lost fellowship	Fellowship restored	- -
Grants "dominion"	Responsibil-ity	Irresponsi-bility	Taking re-sponsibil-ity	To be dominated
Is love	Lives by love	Twists love Hate=inverted love	Restores and perfects love	Responds to tenderness

The lists, of course, go on and on. Notice that what emerges is a comprehensive view of life. Sometimes we assert that "I have my own philosophy of life." Generally, we mean that we have found a way of hooking together the big ideas of life.

Imagine, for a moment, that your basic concepts are a set of lenses. Pretend that they are fastened together into "glasses" through which you look at life. Now, it is obvious that the particular view you have of God affects the "grind" of the lens for each of the other concepts. Even your view of sin will make it necessary to adjust your concept of God and your concept of humanity. You cannot change one concept, you see, without adjusting the other lenses. This simple analogy provides a clue to the reason for the existence of various denominations and theological traditions. Each offers the world a particular vision. It becomes urgent, then, for a congregation to present the clearest set of lenses it can grind. What would be more comic and tragic than for a church to provide one set of lenses through its evangelism and pastoral proclamation and care and a different one through its Christian education curriculum materials?

I have insisted all along that these grand concepts are the guidelines by which decisions are made throughout life. I have raised the question whether teaching facts for the sake of remembering information is very important unless we are helping the child and the growing person to cluster them into concepts. We have observed that facts are remembered longer and more clearly if they are plugged into a meaningful honeycomb--clustered alongside related information. Let us now trace what seems to be the path along which we form a concept, then move to see the concept enlarged into a practical principle, which is put into operation in day-by-day life.

The concept "Christian"

For about two years I have had the pleasure of working occasionally with junior-age children (grades four, five, and six) in a project which may eventually throw light on how attitudes and values are formed, especially with respect to what it means to be a Christian. Before any discussion begins in the experimental unit of study "What Is Christian About Christians?"[3] each child responds to thirty statements describing various feelings toward other people. For each item the child simply indicates "agree" or "disagree." The child's responses give us a profile which seems to reveal to what extent a child's values are rooted in rigid behavioral taboos or in sensitivity to Christian values.

On the thirty-item quiz the child can answer each of the questions in such a way as to affirm or deny that Jesus loves people who use swear words, people who drink beer, people who get killed in accidents resulting from drinking beer, and so forth. The child can affirm or deny that one should be friends with people who hold different values, and that to be Christian is not necessarily to pass judgment on one's neighbors and friends. The child can, further, identify sins of attitude to be equally as serious as those of action.

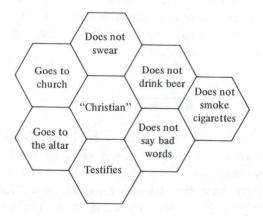

We have now compiled several samples of basic attitudes that make up the child's concept of a Christian. These attitudes are probably acquired accidentally as one observes the behavior of important adult Christians in one's life. It is understandable, then, that in our first efforts to be Christian we assume that those actions are the whole of what it means to be a Christian. Thus, to be a Christian is to do certain things and to avoid doing certain other things. Notice that in this relatively simple actions-make-the-Christian stage of reasoning, there may be no awareness of inward subtleties and motivations at all included in the concept "Christian."

This is, of course, a very limited and flat concept of Christian. One could conclude that such a concept represents only an early stage in understanding, a state through which many Christians pass on their way to a better understanding of Christian. It may be that such a limited concept is most often found in the "child of the church" who grows up observing all of the action of Christians without at the same time having any way of knowing the inward reality of Christian faith. This issue will be explored further in chapter 7. At any rate, it is important to find ways of enhancing the concept of Christian beyond the limited model that is presented.

As a second learning experience in "What Is Christian About Christians?" the children play a game built around identifying five Bible characters. The teacher provides a set of clues, one by one, for the children. The clues are increasingly revealing. When the person is identified, the child is asked to tell other things about the Bible character--things presumably best known and loved by the children. The characters' names are written on the chalkboard, and the children identify each person listed as to whether they are Christians:

Name	Christian	Other
Noah	(X)	X
Pilate		X
Saul (Paul)	X	(X)
Lydia	X	(X)
Jesus	(X)	X

The "Other" category is filled in as accurately as the children can do it. For example, they tend to describe Pilate as "nothing" or as a "Caesar worshiper." When the identity of Saul of Tarsus is guessed from clues before his Christian conversion, he is identified either as a "sinner" or as a "Jew." As the story pushes on, he must be classified after the Damascus Road experience as "Christian." Similarly, double identification comes for Lydia. In all cases we let the children decide from the Bible facts whether the person is a Christian. Classmates are asked to agree or to disagree with an opinion about classification. An informal vote is finally taken to be sure that the children agree.

Whereas the thirty-item questionnaire gave us information about the children's ideas of Christian behavior, this game focuses upon the quality of life of certain Bible people. Now, the concept "Christian" seems to embrace added percepts:

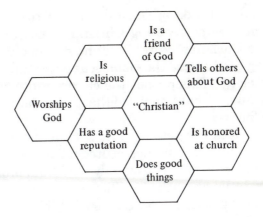

It is here that Saul of Tarsus becomes the center of a problem. Someone invariably observes that he had the best of intentions. Saul meant to *worship God,* to be *religious,* to be a *friend of God,* and to do *good things.* At the same time he was arresting Christians and having them thrown in jail. Can such a man be called a Christian?

The principle: "A Christian is . . ."

It becomes necessary now for the children to go back and add up their percepts again. "What is wrong with our definition? How can we let Saul of Tarsus be a Christian? What have we left out of our definition?"

The children are engaging in the fairly complex process of hypothesis formation. They have had one hypothesis before--made up casually of the sum of their percepts about "Christian." Now, they discover a gap in their thinking. "If Saul was all of these things while he was persecuting Christians, he obviously wasn't a Christian. Why? What made the difference between Saul before the Damascus Road experience and after it?" This pushes the children into asking, specifically, "What happened that made Saul of Tarsus a Christian?"

They check the details in Acts 9:1-6 and discover that the Saul who once persecuted followers of Jesus now called Him "Lord." Not only that, Saul promises to obey Jesus and asked, "What do You want me to do?"[4] Later in the chapter Saul said, "This is the Son of God."[5]

When the children have discovered a defective concept and set about to repair it by filling in more information enlarging the number and richness of their percepts, they are making a *principle*. Principles are well-developed ideas generally consisting of several sub-concepts. They are arrived at by hypothesis formation and hypothesis refinement until the principles stand up satisfactorily under the winds of use, discussion, and opposition.

In the case of the concept "Christian," we have now added two more important restrictions:

When we have added these, our principle reads something like this: "A Christian is a person who (1) believes in Jesus as God and obeys Him, (2) has been forgiven for his sins, and (3) tells others about Jesus Christ the Lord."

With this refined hypothesis we are in trouble on Noah, for the children unwittingly classified him as Christian. The question of historical timing comes up. "If Noah had lived when Jesus was alive, Noah would have been a Christian," one young man said. "But he had to be something else." He finally suggested, "a God believer . . . does that make him a God-ian?"

Finally, "Was Jesus a Christian?" must be reconsidered. "No, He didn't need a Savior. He was God." So we change the earlier classifications to meet the narrower limits of our latest hypothesis. We are well on our way to the development of a high quality principle.

Whereas the percepts "Believe in Jesus" and "Says Christ is Lord!" are foundation stones in building an adequate concept of Christian and in forming a working principle, "A Christian is . . .," the comprehensive principle must cover a great deal more than expected actions (the first percepts we looked at) and the required beliefs (examined with Saul). We still have no working principle that copes with inward attitudes, values, and choices.

So, a final exploration must be made in which children learn to thoroughly evaluate Christian attitudes and their resulting actions and compare them with samples of attitudes and the resulting actions they see in their own lives. We will look at the attitudes of Jesus toward sinners and victims of sin. Then we will pose problems from our own times and test our feelings about the people involved. When we have discovered that being a Christian is basically a matter of being made over with new attitudes and of keeping those attitudes alive by consistently expressing them in behavior, then we will be ready to draw up a working definition in which we set forth "What Is Christian About Christians."

Looking back from principle to facts

It takes a great deal of experience, a sea of facts to sort and file, and considerable time for concepts to form into clusters and for concepts to build into working principles. Once a principle has been formed and tested in a variety of circumstances it becomes as treasured and useful as a long and cherished friendship.

When we examine the shape of our present concepts in the light of our past understandings, we are frequently surprised to find that the facts which went into the concepts forming a philosophy of life are not easy to recall. They may exist only as an irretrievable part of that strong fabric of the soul that makes us distinctly who we are. They may even have been replaced by wider and more useful ways of interpreting events. For example, instead of compartments reading "No smoking," "No drinking," we may now have a larger section reading "Shows respect for human life, including our own. Abstains from harmful consumption, including overeating; practices physical fitness for the body, which is the temple of the Holy Spirit." The taboo compartments that were useful to us in the years of our beginning understanding are too narrow and too brittle to cover the height and depth of human responsibility they stood for long ago in our experience.

7

Knowing by Feeling
What You Do

Mary Elizabeth Sergent tells the story of Tom and
Sue Smith and their two children. Both Tom and Sue
were dedicated as infants; both attended Sunday school.
Their first child, Dick, was also properly baptized at
six weeks. When he was five, they put him in Sunday
school. A neighbor who attended their church always
took him. Dickie wasn't too fond of Sunday school.
Then, with a tiny baby sister in the house, the family
moved. Tom's business and his golf consumed all of his
time. They sent the children to a nearby church and
did make it for the Christmas pageant and for Children's Day. Sue thought the Children's Day program
was terrible; she had been a teacher herself, and poor
programs were inexcusable. The pastor's wife asked
her to take a class. "Oh, I really couldn't." With PTA
and Red Cross, she couldn't consider it. She confessed
ignorance of the Bible. "It's so dull." And take Dickie's
class? "I couldn't keep discipline with boys." Tom?
"Oh, mercy no! He isn't interested in religion." She
wished the minister's wife would leave. Some of her
friends were coming in for cocktails, and she was
dying for a smoke.

Several boys in Dick's Sunday school class were

*joining the church. He missed the first of six member-
ship classes. His mother covered for him: "He has so
many activities, and he belongs to a little club that
meets Friday nights." He never did join the church.
Camping kept him out of church many Sundays. But
young Ann insisted she wanted to be baptized. (Tom
and Sue had been too busy ever to have her baptized as
a baby in their old church.) Tom and Dick had other
plans for Easter.*

*In the end Sue went alone to witness Ann's baptism.
She gave Ann a gold cross as a memento. Ann had a
date that night, and the next communion Sunday they
were at their lake cottage, so between one thing and
another Ann never did go through with church membership, either.*

*World War II came. Dick enlisted and landed in
Ireland. Ann, still in college, eloped with a boy she had
met at a USO dance. Six months later Tom and Sue
were grandparents. The doctor said the baby was
premature.*

*Dick wrote from Ireland that he was in love. His girl
was praying for him; he felt he would be safe in France.
Tom said that was a laugh--anyone praying for Dick.
Sue didn't say anything.*

*Dick did come through the war. He married his girl
and brought her home. He joined the Catholic Church.
"I figured what my kids were going to be, I might as
well be, too."*

*Ann's husband survived, too, but their marriage
didn't. Her husband fell for a pretty WAC in Manila.
He developed the same kind of love for her he had
shown toward Ann. Ann is divorced now, working in*

New York--a brilliant but brittle woman, cynical and bitter, and an outspoken atheist.

On Easter and Christmas Sue still goes to church. She still works at the Red Cross but feels "women's work is deadly routine, except for the children." And both of hers are a deep disappointment to her.

Tom is disappointed, too. "I can't understand it," he complains to Sue. "With all the advantages of a good home and a Christian community, why didn't they grow up to be good, decent Protestants like you and me?"[1]

Learning that precedes teaching

Most of us know, although we may behave as if we did not, that a great deal of learning may occur when no conscious teaching is going on. We could call it "the hidden curriculum." We know our informal modeling and teaching is "the real curriculum." The irate father, upon learning that his son has been involved in a fight, takes him to the basement and beats him violently, all the while muttering, "Haven't I taught you better than to get in a fight?" Obviously not. Quite the opposite, the father has taught the son that violence is the way we demonstrate who is bigger and who is littler. Big and strong people can use violence on weaker ones.

Consider the mystery of learning in early childhood. By the time children arrive in their first class at school, they have picked up a workable grasp of one of the most complicated things in the world--their native language. They have done with it what they will probably never do with another language in years of formal study. Besides language, they have mastered essential social habits, acquired a fairly complex set of right and wrong values, and are skillful interpreters of the attitudes and moods of other people. They have done all of this without reading a single word, attending a class, or taking a test. They have gained more knowledge before they start to school, someone has suggested, than they will accumulate in four years of college.

We must be attentive to our children, then, when they look up quizzically and beg to be let off having to recite an answer, saying, "How can I know what I think until I feel what I do?" They may not say it aloud. But you might remember that their most enduring and enjoyable learning was that which came with total immersion in an environment. Then, you could take steps to help them "feel the doing" of what you want to share with them.

Development and Learning

The best insights available to us in the psychology of child development suggest that children move through perhaps three or four critical stages between toddlerhood and adulthood. That is, you could group a wide age span of children into only a very few groups if you were grouping them by their developmental needs. We have come to suppose that every year in a child's life poses a new crisis, so we have imagined that teaching could only be at its best if we segregated children into one-year groups.

As a matter of fact, children learn a great deal from each other, and it could be argued that where ideas and concepts are under exploration the very best grouping would throw learners of various ages together. Then too, in the church we are interested in creating a learning fellowship that transcends tight one-year loyalties. Children who move up through a Sunday school always with children their own age miss cultivating understanding and friendship with persons older and younger. On the other hand, a child who moves through a group-graded system, or open-graded, or even intergenerational environment develops bonds of learning fellowship with both older and younger persons. For example, even in a small church where there are only three classes in the junior department (grades four, five, and six), it should be seriously considered whether the purposes of Christian education might not be better fulfilled if the children were grouped in mixed-age classes instead of isolated into single-year grades.

Not only do the insights of Piaget, Erikson, Havighurst, and Kohlberg push us toward ministering to the needs of children in developmental groups, they also support the notion that the ways of learning and knowing are essentially the same regardless of age. If it is true that the ways of knowing are universal in all age-groups, then it is perhaps our most urgent task to discover those ways and develop skill in using them with all learning situations. Jerome Bruner has identified three ways that a learner may encounter things to be learned.[2]

We will call these three ways of knowing *action, image,* and *words.* I remember listening to a conversation as an energetic Christian was trying to persuade a relatively new friend to become a Christian. The main line of attack was, "Don't you see, you're a sinner, and what you need to do is to make your confession and be justified before God." The paralyzed victim heard every syllable, but the words made no contact with his reality. The abstract words being used had no significant meaning to him. Bruner's "ways of knowing" help us to see the full spectrum ranging from very specific and concrete ways of knowing all the way to tight verbal abstractions. Of the "three ways of knowing," it may be that one or both of the other ways of knowing might have connected with the bewildered "sinner's" understanding and led to a very different and more appropriate response.

The feel of doing

Knowing by *action* refers to learning by doing something. You might write a book on how to throw a curve ball in baseball (or on the steps to being converted to Christian faith), but I will grasp it more quickly if you show me how your hand grasps the ball. Then, give me a slow-motion demonstration of what you do with your wrist and fingers and let me feel the ball myself, and I will be on my way to being a pitcher. You have represented a curve ball pitch to me by action. Most of us do not remember the first time we tried to place a key into a lock, had trouble getting it in, and finally felt a big hand enclosing ours and lifting the whole little hand with its key until at the correct altitude and angle the entrance was made. We felt the turn of the lock tumblers and walked through the door. Once was enough. But you can't learn it from a book. Think of the vast storehouse of knowledge that you acquired because it was represented for you by action: how to ride a bicycle, tie your shoes, and on and on.

Now, in the church we are not generally teaching lock manipulation or ball throwing, but action learning still holds as a highly effective means of teaching. This is no plea for activity for the sake of activity. Instead, we must look for every opportunity to demonstrate ideas rather than merely to tell or to furnish reading material. Think of the action learning strategies you might use to teach these concepts and skills:

How to find the Acts of the Apostles
How to pray
Reverence
The meaning of baptism
Patience
Forgiveness
Repentance

We talk a great deal about forgiveness. Yet, many children have not developed a clear concept for the word. The concept will become clear, however, with a brief time of role playing:

Teacher: I am asking Jack and Jim to play a game for us. Jack and Jim often play together. Jack has a new book his grandfather gave him. One day he shows it to Jim. Jim is careless and tears one of the big picture pages almost out of the book. How will Jack feel? How will Jim feel? Let's have them play out their feelings.

Here, the teacher asks Jack and Jim to walk side by side across the room, not talking, but walking heavily and looking sad. They walk, heads down. Jim rubs his eyes. The teacher wonders whether Jim is really crying, but it becomes evident that he is only feeling his role seriously.

Teacher: Now, let us ask Jack and Jim to talk about the torn book. Jack, you begin. It was your book.

Jack: You tore my book, and it was brand new.

Jim: I didn't mean to do it.

Jack: I'm going to make you pay for it.

Jim: I wish I could. Do you think we could fix it?

Jack: It would never be like new.

Jim: I'm awfully sorry. Will you forgive me?

Jack: I don't know. I guess so, if you'll help me fix it.

Teacher: Now, do you think it is harder to ask for forgiveness or to forgive? *(Here the concept begins to come into focus.)*

The entire story "Why Aren't They Like Us?" is essentially an account of parents who assumed that they were not teaching, but, in fact, were. With action teaching we are offering the learners the feel of doing. They are drawn into our action and get the feel of our way of behaving. They may then say, "If I like the way it feels, I will make it a part of me." It may be, however, that learners have no alternative but to imitate the acted-out teachings of important people in their lives. Children learn their actions by home practice. In the church we may be able to offer alternatives, but the major influence of actions and words comes from the family. It will be important that workers in the church are intentional about their "action teaching" in their limited contact with children and youth.

Consider, for example, the peril that confronts us if what we live (act out) does not ring true to what we say. The learner has to choose then between ignoring us altogether or assuming that what we say and what we do have no direct relation to each other. The first response will empty the church in short order; the second will populate it with well-indoctrinated carbon copies of their hypocritical teachers. Indeed, doctrine consistently refers to action in the New Testament. So to "do theology" is to live and learn the meaning of God's way with us.

Images that teach

You might try to teach me how to throw a curve ball by drawing me a picture. You could show me the kinds of paths a pitched ball might take. You could draw a picture of fingers gripping the ball and draw lines to indicate the motion necessary to deliver the curve.

You might even go to the trouble of preparing a motion picture for me to watch so that the pictures could stick in my head as I tried my luck at home. Neither of these visual representations gets to my muscles quite like your "action teaching." With action, you let me get the feel of holding the ball properly and releasing it at the right time.

A picture of a thing is not the real thing, but it stands for reality in this kind of learning with images. Consider, for example, how we might learn about forgiveness by using pictures:

These boys are separated because of a torn page in a prized book. Jim feels bad because he has torn the book. Jack feels bad because it was his treasured book. The hurt feelings are represented by the lines through the heads of the boys. A wall of "hurt" keeps them apart. It is not going to be easy for either of them to get the wall down. Both of them will have to suffer if they are to be friends again. Both will have to cooperate to take down the wall:

The problem that divides the boys will have to be faced squarely. They must find some way to agree on what to do about the book. As Jim finds a way to show that he is sorry that he tore the book, Jack must find a way to forgive Jim and save the friendship. The hurt feelings begin to leave as the friendship is saved, but it is a hard job for both boys, and the book will never be the same again. Forgiveness is not easy.

Knowing by words

Language sets humans apart from all other living things. It may account in large part for the rise of civilization. By the use of words we tell our history to our young. We do this by making written records, of course, but mostly by telling our story to our children.

When we get right down to it, language evidently is deeply rooted in action. There are words in every language that suggest by their sound the action they are describing: *spit, crunch, sigh,* for example. Several languages have retained an essentially picture (image) form for writing. Then, too, if we use a metaphor, which creates images in the mind, we might be said to be using images, though the means (words) would be symbolic. For the most part, the words we use are pulled loose from their action and image origins. They are only sounds that have agreed-upon meanings among people. They are symbols used to communicate rapidly and flexibly with other people.

In the church we have tended to assume that the world could be saved through words. We have talked, lectured, and preached. We possess very abstract ideas--the great Christian truths. But we have tried to share those highly symbolic ideas almost exclusively by the use of still other abstract symbols-- arbitrary "Readers' Digest" words. It is as if the coming generation had complained that they could not understand our cumbersome encyclopedias and we responded by writing them a set of dictionaries. What they needed in their childhood were images and actions to give shape to the ideas we wished to share with them.

The modern ideas of *preaching, teaching,* and *witnessing* are almost entirely limited to *talking.* It has not always been so. Noah preached righteousness by action. Ezekiel dramatized the tragic condition of his people and spoke in colorful images and pantomimes. Jesus' best remembered sermons were those shared out of doors in action settings. Indeed, the acid test of Jesus' doctrine, He said, was the test of "doing it."

Read John 7:17 in two or three translations: "If anyone chooses to do [action!] God's will, that person will find out whether my teaching comes from God or whether I am speaking [words!] on my own." Most of what is remembered about what He said is recorded in word pictures-the parables and stories He used. Many of these stories must have been told on the spot as they were being lived out within view--the sower, the lilies, and the sheep, for example.

The word from which we get "witness" is the same word as that for "martyr." In the early church a witness was one who testified for Jesus, especially by death. One's courageous living gave the words special meaning.

We may have misunderstood the profound idea behind "Word" as a name for Jesus. It is true that John the Baptist called himself "the voice." He spoke of one coming after him (called "the Word"). And the writer of Hebrews carried the idea further: "When in former times God spoke to our forefathers, he spoke in fragmentary and varied fashion through the prophets. But in this the final age [God] has spoken to us in the Son whom he has made heir to the whole universe, and through whom he created all orders of existence: the Son who is the effulgence of God's splendour and the stamp of God's very being, and sustains the universe by his word of power."[3] Notice that God *spoke;* God *spoke* through prophets; God has *spoken* in His Son; the universe is sustained by the *word* of His power. The Gospel by John gives Jesus His classic identity: "the Word."

God has not made our error, however. He has not

talked people to death. There is action in creation; there is image in incarnation and redemption; and there is an entire life lived out in the most unparalleled enactment of love the world has ever seen--the life, suffering, and death of our Lord. Jesus Christ put more stock in action and parables (pictures) than in highly symbolic language as a means of getting to the persons who were in desperate need of Him. Indeed both Mark and Matthew report that Jesus never taught the crowds without a parable, and only in the smaller circle did He explain everything with abstract words. Look at those statements in Mark 4:33-34 and Matthew 13:34. Surely we can choose the most effective ways of knowing to share our ideas with people who are now in need.

When we examine the roles played in learning by action, image, and word, we are confronted with searching questions: What are the actions by which the church is already teaching effectively? Can they be conserved and expanded? Consider the few kinds of action teaching that are scheduled in the church: kneeling as an act of adoration to Christ; public personal response in Christian commitment; public taking of vows to Christ and the church; observance of baptism and of the Lord's Supper: and the presentation of tithes and offerings.

Can we develop action teaching for each of the grand ideas of the Christian faith? Is it true that a child sees and is attracted to the love of Christ which shines through a Sunday school teacher? If so, can this "hidden" and even accidental part of the curriculum be expanded and cultivated on purpose? If forgiveness is a crucial concept, how can it be learned from action experience?

How can we develop "image" teachings for each of our great concepts? We are quick to use the simple picture--a realistic representation of a person or an event. How shall we go about putting *ideas* into images?

Once we are prepared to translate the good news into actions and images to support our verbal (word) teaching, we must acknowledge additional concern. How can we go beyond teaching ideas and concepts to help people make responsible decisions? That is, how can we help people turn what they know into decisive action? Only when learning is translated into life can we be assured that we have been really successful in our teaching.

8

Teaching for Decision Making

"Now, here we have Paul and his evangelistic party trying to find where it is that God wants them to go next." A teacher of young teenagers moved into the problem phase of his class discussion. "They have had clear direction from the Holy Spirit not to go into Bithynia--up toward Byzantium, the modern Istanbul. Notice the problem: How do we find out what God wants us to do and where He wants us to go next? That is a pretty universal kind of question. All of us face it several times in our lives.

"Finally, Paul and his friends stop at Troas. They have worked up the western coast of what is now modern Turkey. They may have stopped at many of the Christian communities mentioned in Revelation-- Laodicea, Philadelphia, Sardis, Ephesus, Smyrna, Thyatira, and Pergamum. Troas was the city Homer called Troy. Remember hearing tales about 'Helen of Troy'? People who lived in Troy were called Trojans. You can see from its location that it was a strategic city. It guarded the Dardanelles, the straits through which ships of trade and war had to pass to get to Byzantium (Istanbul) and to the Black Sea.

"It is here, then, that Paul awakens in the night with

a vision. God is finally going to tell him what to do. In the vision, a man says to Paul, 'Come over into Macedonia, and help us.' The story is in Acts 16. Immediately, Paul and his party obeyed and sailed across the northeast end of the Aegean Sea. They bypassed the province of Thrace and came to Philippi. There they touched off a Christian movement that eventually spread over all of western Europe. Now, here is the question I want you to talk about for a few minutes: What difference does it make to you that Paul waited to know God's plan for him, and then was obedient to the call of God?"

For a few seconds the students reflect on the glimpse into Paul's preaching career and on the question the teacher has posed. Then one student says:

"Well, maybe we wouldn't be here, or at least we wouldn't be us. I mean, North America was settled mostly by people from western Europe. And if they hadn't been influenced by Christianity, they probably wouldn't have been very civilized. I think somebody else would have discovered and settled America."

Another student volunteered. "Europe might still be inhabited by savage tribes just now having civil wars to establish their nations, like is happening in Africa and parts of Asia."

"If Paul had gone east instead of west," another teenager offered, "it's possible that we would be hearing the gospel from the Chinese today. They might be sending missionaries to us. Who knows? India and Russia might be the predominantly Christian countries today."

"All right," the teacher interrupted, "I think we agree

that a great many features of our history have been affected by the fact that Christianity spread west into Europe. It is also pretty clear that the direction of its spread was the result of the obedience of one man who tried very hard to know what God wanted him to do. Let me ask you some other questions: What difference will it make five years from now whether or not you find the will of God and respond to it? What difference do you see, then, in ten years? In twenty-five years? What difference may it make one hundred years from now whether you lived in faith and obedience to God?"

At this point the teacher has skillfully led the young people into a series of questions that have a moral dimension. Effective teachers can do it without using religious gimmicks. Our teacher here has not resorted to making judgmental statements about the students' personal relationships to God. In the church we are intent on developing decision-making skills. Here are some of the issues involved in building for decision making.

Fact + fact = concept

In chapters 4 and 5 we explored the role of factual information in building the abiding concepts that carry us through life. We suggested, for example, that it is not easy to hold a bit of factual information in place in one's head unless it is welded to other information by some relationship. The fact "Paul had a vision at Troas" may be memorized and held in mind by the sounds of the statement. It would be better held in mind if the piece of information were welded to other facts: Troas is the ancient city of Troy. Troy was located at the Dardanelles, the western gateway to the Sea of Marmara. At the east end of the Sea of Marmara is Istanbul, the ancient city of Byzantium or Constantinople. After the vision Paul sailed northwest toward upper Greece, to Philippi. He left Asia (by crossing the Dardanelles) and entered Europe.

By the time Paul's decision is related to this geography we have the raw material for several concepts:

Troas (or Troy)
Europe
Asia
called by God
missionary to Europe

We may have others. On the other hand, it is virtually impossible to hold Paul's vision at Troas in mind for any meaningful purpose unless it is held in terms of these concepts.

When you break down the possible kinds of mental activities humans can perform, the simplest one is sometimes called "cognition."[1] If you "cognize," it only means you are alert, that you recognize events, people, and facts; you know them as you would recognize a person. As they file past, you nod to them and say, "Yes, I recognize you, and you, and you. . . ." At the cognition level you make no effort to remember them.

If you wanted to remember the "cognitions," you would have to memorize them. You could not memorize nine million a day--one estimate of the number you process in a typical day--but you could select a few to remember. Consider your own experience in meeting a group of persons unknown to you. You process their names: Thomas Jones, William Brown, Eugene Johnson, Joseph Adams, and so forth. The names have a familiar sound. You nod to each person and say, "I am pleased to meet you." You know that tomorrow there will be a new set of names and faces; you will no longer need to know these people. But, suppose that you will be seeing these people not only tomorrow but also for many months afterward. *I must remember their names,* you say to yourself. So you begin inventing categories; you begin welding names and faces to existing frames of reference in your head. You will invent your own rules for this game; no one else will ever know: Jones = keen eyed as my college friend Jones + Thomas, my younger brother's middle name, and so on. The welding process continues. You will use the temporary cues until you have better material to which to weld the name--the new acquaintance's own characteristics and your meaningful experiences with the person Thomas Jones.

Memorization, like cognition, is a fairly low-level mental operation. It requires only that you sort out certain cognitions and hold them in mind for later use. The diplomas on our shelves represent the fact that we were successful in remembering some of the most wanted facts long enough to feed them back to our instructors. In the church, however, the motivations for memorization are related to other kinds of rewards than diplomas or grades.[2] Handling facts and

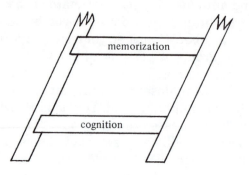

memorizing are fairly complex tasks. They are also essential for any rich learning adventure. But they do not get us into the mental activities that are directly involved in decision making.

Right-answer thinking

There are at least two ways of looking at how we solve problems. We could take the view that there is one right answer for any given problem and our task consists of finding that answer. The other view would be that it is not always easy to find the best, most efficient answer for many problems and that it requires imagination, flexibility, and rich use of one's resources to cope with problems. The first of these views calls for "convergent thinking." It suggests that all roads lead at last to one answer. Theoretically, if there is a given right answer for any question, that answer could be known if one had learned enough facts and had memorized them. In the church we deal with a great many right-answer decisions. We begin with certain *givens*. For example, there are the Ten Commandments. They seem to be clear statements on moral issues. They are part of the Word of God, which is timeless and authoritative. That Word can be applied to any human situation at any time in history; it can be generalized to any specific setting and to all kinds of human relationships. Profanity, stealing, lust, infidelity, and greed are wrong; they are wrong wherever they are found and whoever is involved. These are givens. The teachings of Jesus also intersect our lives on specific issues. So, for a large number of questions we have the right answer. But for a large proportion of our questions there is no clearly black or white category. The Ten Commandments condemn stealing, but how does one solve the problem of sloth? How do you keep yourself sensitive to the obligation to deliver a full eight-hours' worth of work or imagination every day to your employer? Furthermore, although you may have memorized a formula which defines stealing as contrary to the will of God, how do you make it your very own internal standard? How is decision making different from mere knowledge of the moral right and wrong?

One may gather facts and develop a set of rules, even memorize them, but if the mental processing of that information does not require a personal moral choice, it may be that no moral decision has been made. For example, one might be able to recite not only the Ten Commandments but also the Apostles' Creed verbatim. These documents are full of theologically and morally correct statements. If we have memorized them, we could furnish many right answers to anyone who wished to test us. But there may be a wide gulf between what we are able to recite and what we actually feel and practice. If I am asked to affirm my belief in the bodily resurrection of Jesus Christ so that I may belong to the church, please the minister, or keep face with my friends at church, I am placed in a convergent choice bind. I can give the right answer, but it may not be given with conviction. I have not considered the alternatives. To do that I will have to wrestle with the possibility that humans die as do the animals and return to be one with the earth. If this were true, it would mean not that I am created for two worlds, but that I am the product and the captive of one. I will then contemplate the significance of the claims that one Man entered into human existence, died, and reversed the processes common to animals. Jesus Christ is offered to me as the solitary piece of evidence that I am a creature of two worlds and that I, too, am called to eternal life with Him. When one has contemplated these issues, it is not easy to be indifferent to the implications of "I believe in the resurrection of the dead." One will want either to silence the lips so as to avoid speaking a fraud or to affirm the Resurrection with confident vigor.

Convergent thinking, while useful to us in defining a set of correct beliefs and guidelines, may be deadly if we apply it to all learning in the church. When teaching is dogmatic and authoritarian, the church tends to suffer from a right-answer syndrome. We create the false impression that there are right answers for every issue. A Sunday school teacher may feel obligated to close the door on questioning. Any of us may be inclined to "drive home the truth" of our own ideas or of official Christian belief. In other words, dogmatism as a way of life may grow up among persons in the church if we stop all mental processes at the right-answer level. If we do so, we not only blight the personal and spiritual growth of persons (which may well be a form of sinning against the Holy Spirit whose temple they are), but we forfeit life, vitality, and creativity that can flourish only as people are continually alert in identifying new problems and in searching for appropriate ways to respond to their demands.

Creative problem solving

Convergent thinking skills are particularly useful in stripping away the false and arriving at the true. When the problem one faces, however, is more complex than sorting truth from error, a different set of skills may be needed. Divergent thinking, in contrast to convergent skills, is that mental activity which moves about freely in search of workable hypotheses to apply to complicated problems. With divergent thinking we stress the importance of spontaneous ideas, mixing known facts with new problems not always related in any visible way. We ask the person to tackle the problem in a unique and personal way. We show respect for innovation and for creative ideas, rejecting nothing at first impulse. We prime the

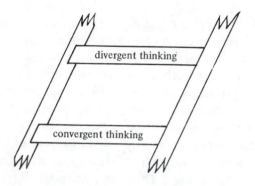

mysterious pump from which flow fresh and personal ideas. The teacher of young teenagers might have asked several convergent questions during the session on Paul at Troas. The teacher could have asked, for example, "What was the old name for Troas, which we know from the history of great military heroes and battles?" There is only one right answer: He left Troas by boat for Philippi, making intermediate stops at the ports of Samothracia and Neapolis. These are particularly good questions to use, if you are wanting to be sure that your students are covering the ground with you.

You may feel, however, that there is something more important to do. You may fear that your students may feed back right answers and still fall short of your goals for them in a given session. If so, you might use divergent questioning. When the teacher asked the teenagers, "What difference does it make to you that Paul was obedient to the call of God?" the students were facing a divergent question. You see at once that there are likely to be as many responses to that question as there are students in the class. Each student brings to bear on the question all the retrieveable factual material from the class experience and from an entire lifetime of sorting and filing meaningful information. Every student can quickly produce a combination from these resources, cross-reference them, and form a tentative hypothesis to share with the rest of us. It is virtually impossible for a person to answer questions in a divergent questioning experience without making moral judgments--without cultivating the art of decision making.

Divergent thinking requires that a person relate the present problem to the full backlog of life's learning and experience. Since one of the most severe charges that can be made against any educational institution is that it is irrelevant, in the church we must cultivate procedures that will help us use our knowledge and experience to solve problems. These will help us to break "religion" and "life" out of their airtight compartments as the total resources of each are brought to bear upon the real problem of both.

When Jesus said, "I am ... truth," and again, "You shall know the truth, and the truth shall make you free,"[3] He was evidently serious about the necessity of our working to unravel all kinds of mysteries about this do-it-yourself planet and about the nature of humanity and the nature of God. Paul, wrestling with the vastness of the concepts of the nature of God and of truth, observed that Jesus Christ "is the image of the invisible God; his is the primacy over all created things. In him everything in heaven and on earth was created . . . : the whole universe has been created through him and for him. And he exists before every-

thing, and all things are held together in him."[4]
Again, the teacher suggested that in Christ "lie hidden all God's treasures of wisdom and knowledge."[5]
Christian truth, then, is no shaky invention needing our propping up or our overprotective defense. Instead, one might say that investigation is invited. Lift the test tube! Collect the data! When the evidence is all in, it will testify of Jesus; all truth ultimately has its root in Him. Real life and ultimate truth are harmonious. Where else can one find a more balanced view of the nature of humanity and of the world?

Developing decision makers

Notice the improved quality of thinking at each of the steps we have traced. One needs only to be conscious and able to follow the sounds of the teacher's voice with understanding to engage in "cognition." In memorization we slow down some of the millions of cognitions that whiz past our senses; we single them out to remember and to weld them to something already in our minds. In "convergent thinking" learners sort and narrow the alternatives logically until they can give the right answer. In "divergent thinking" we bring all our knowledge and experience to bear upon solving a problem; as we do so, we wrestle with the value of the alternatives as well as the logic of them. Now, in "evaluative thinking" we see the learner confronted with having to decide what *ought* to be done. The learner must say what is right morally, not just what is right logically. One needs a great

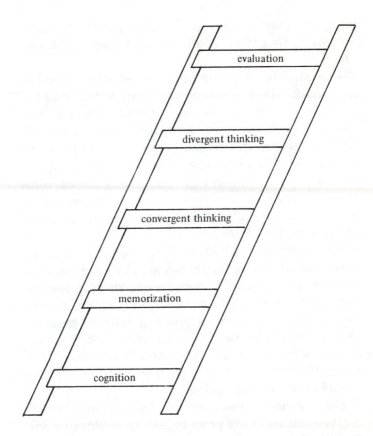

many facts to make a moral judgment, but facts alone will not suffice. Your moral judgment expressed in words and in daily choices is the product of your conscience--your internalized values. These have been defined as the "store of sound and socially responsible beliefs and convictions" which you possess. "Decision making requires more than mere knowledge of facts and principles; it requires a weighing in the balance, a synthesizing of all available information and values."[6]

In evaluative thinking Christian education reaches its climax. The Christian faith is essentially an expression of a particular set of values. Its chief evidence in one's life is in the transformation of one's "store of sound and socially responsible beliefs and convictions." The Christian person is not merely involved in making basic right and wrong choices common to everyone; the Christian is a re-created person with an increasingly higher awareness of the moral implications of all problems.

For example, the Paul-at-Troas decision might be looked on as a mere business game by a merchant of oriental goods. But Paul faced it as a moral question, because he saw bound up with it the issues of life and death. He could not go on with any sense of meaning in his life unless he had assurance that God was directing his activities. And the life and death fortunes of other persons depended on whether he found and obeyed the will of God.

Our teacher of teenagers led the students through a divergent thinking process into an evaluative one: "What difference may it make one hundred years from now whether you lived in faith and obedience to God?" By the time his students have explored the implications of his questions, they will not only have developed a set of principles from their discoveries, but they will also have made moral judgments in their own minds. Their facts will have yielded these principles, all with moral dimensions:

1. God has specific plans for people.
2. God has plans for nations--groups of people.
3. Sometimes these plans depend on each other.
4. If history is good, it is because people made good decisions.
5. If history is bad, it is probably because people made bad decisions.

It is clear, then, that the quality of our decisions is directly related to what we know. It is also clear that the urgency of decision making forces us to collect additional information and reorganize old knowledge to bring needed resources together for problem solving. If you have to make a decision, you will be more alert to facts and details having a bearing on that decision than you will be if you face no decision and are asked only to sit still and remember what is being thrown at you.

What is more, the quality of decisions that will be made depends upon whether we have developed skills that bring together our fund of facts with our store of sound, responsible, thoroughly Christian beliefs and convictions. Tomorrow's world will confront us all with issues more complex than the already terrifying agenda of today. We could not possibly hope to pass on to our children enough specific rules to guide them through the uncharted seas ahead. If they find, however, that in the loving environment of the church and home they are encouraged to try their skills in making choices and testing hypotheses, they will be well prepared to go out into tomorrow.

How are these "thoroughly Christian beliefs and convictions," which they so badly need, to be acquired? Can morality be taught? How does one's conscience get its shape, anyway? These are perhaps the climactic questions confronting us in our quest for making learning in the church meaningful. To these we must turn next.

9

How Are Values Formed?

When Dick Smith married outside his faith and his sister, Ann, divorced her husband and retreated to the bitterness of atheism, they were living out their own real values.[1]

Values have been defined as one's "store of sound and socially responsible beliefs and convictions."[2] The working beliefs and convictions that Dick and Ann adopted took them away from the professed values of their parents. It seems to have been a case in which the parents' real beliefs overpowered their imagined beliefs, and the children took the real instead of the professed values for their own. Indeed, one could even say that the children were more praiseworthy than their parents; the children at least lived out the barefaced implications of their lack of faith, whereas the parents maintained a facade of Christianity.

We are attentive to Dick and Ann Smith just now because they represent a large number of children who come under the influence of the educational ministry of the church. Among the things we need to know is whether, or to what extent, the church can contribute to the shaping of values, especially in the young. One's conscience seems to be the product of many forces: parents, relatives, age-mates, school instruction, church teaching, one's own insight and constructions of "reality," self- discipline, and strength of will. Conscience development is a subject not widely explored by research, but some evidence has been collected that can serve to guide us.

Conscience: mark of humanity

Humans have the longest childhood among all creatures on earth (except elephants). We are also alone in using a complicated language to communicate with others. The biblical idea suggests that the universe was called into existence by a speaking God[3] who created a speaking man. By means of our language we pass on a heritage, so each child is born with the legacy of several thousand years of experience and its wisdom. There is a sense in which the human conscience is the effect that follows as we make our history a guiding part of ourselves. Most often we take it in just as it is fed to us by important people in our life experience. But regardless of what we internalize or where we got the ideas we swallowed, we possess a sense of goodness and badness that affects our relationships to other people and with the entire ecosystem--"the earth" and the universe. One depth psychologist calls this moral sense the "super ego" or the internalized parent. But a Swiss epistemologist playing marbles in the street with children found that they apparently are born with an innate sense of justice. And at Harvard, yet another researcher now has isolated justice in women facing abortion decisions and calls it "attachment."

The human conscience is evidently universally and intrinsically present in every person. The "image of God" consisting of righteousness and true holiness surely reflects God's "steadfast love." I wrestled with the "image of God" concept in *The Holy Spirit and You*. So, suddenly there is no surprise that Christian education consists of the care and nurture of the image of God. The image of God is established by the "breath of God" at Cre-ation and remains to respond to Him in all of us if we are open to God's filling with His breath. I have explored this developmental model of moral and ethical development in *Moral Development Foundations*.

The pressure of age-mates

Sociologists remind us that there are complicated peer cultures in America. For example, there are cultures in your community that correspond to departments you have in your Sunday school: primary, junior, young teen, senior teen, young adult, and senior adult. Each "kid culture" in which our young move is a system. Christian education environments create a system which grants each member some specific status, value, and role. A typical person, counting family, extended family, and these systems, tends to live and move in about five significant systems. We tend to abandon any system in which our status, value, and role are trivialized or are insignificant or "shame" based.

Some of the most interesting research dealing with the influence of age-mates on children is only partially reported to the public now; it comes from Cornell University. Several researchers compared 150 Russian children with 150 American children to see whether one group was more willing than the other to violate a moral code. The results indicated that, on the whole, American children "were far more ready to take part in such actions."[4]

When children were told that their peers would know about their morally disapproved behavior (such as cheating on a test or denying responsibility for property damage), the American children were even more willing to transgress. The Soviet children showed just the opposite tendency. "The peer group operated to support the values of the adult society, at least at their age level." The report says that in Russia the child's "collective" or school peer group is held responsible for the actions and morality of its members. In contrast, in America "the peer group is often an autonomous agent relatively free from adult control and uncommitted--if not outrightly opposed--to the values and codes of conduct approved by society at large." Any way you interpret the results, there is strong evidence that age-mate influence is very powerful. If we remember that there may be more rewards in "role, status, and value or significance" in a destructive peer system than we are offering in church-based relationships, we may want to study our strategies to make them more systemically magnetic.

Some American authorities feel that the school should be given full responsibility for shaping the values (consciences) of American young people. One of them, James S. Coleman, dismisses the American home as having any potential for shaping its young. He takes this view in spite of the fact that his own research shows that the home holds about a 10 percent edge over age-mates in influencing adolescents not to participate in a morally wrong action.[5]

Early indications from an experiment with middle elementary children in Sunday school settings show that age-mate opinion is important. As the children work together in class to decide on appropriate action in cases of moral choice, they seem to depend on each other a great deal in deciding what is right and wrong.[6]

Parents and values

The biblical idea of conscience development is that parents are responsible both for the moral instruction and for the moral behavior of the child. The ancient Hebrew creed is set in the middle of instructions to parents on how to make their teaching effective and meaningful to children. Those instructions in Deuteronomy 6:1-9 call for *action, image,* and *word* kinds of teaching.[7] *Action:* The adult generation was to "observe to do" God's command, leading to material blessing (6:3). *Image:* The adult generation was to "bind [God's law] for a sign" upon their hands and between their eyes, and they were to write His law upon the posts of their houses and on their gates (6:8-9). The visual representations stood for the real thing before its meaning was understood by the children. *Words:* "Thou shalt teach them diligently unto thy children, and shalt talk of them when thou sittest in thine house, and when thou walkest by the way, and when thou liest down, and when thou risest up" (6:7). This massive program of religious education was to be motivated by having God's words in the heart, and presumably the education was for the singular purpose of leading the children to *internalize* that beloved word in the same way: "These words . . . shall be in thine heart" (6:6).

Most of the early research about conscience development has grown out of psychoanalytic theory. That research has tried to trace the imitation patterns of children as they relate to one or both parents. This led, naturally, to efforts to discover how a child forms his values. For example, classical studies at Stanford University looked at the strength of conscience in young children who are confronted with a contrived temptation. In one of the experiments a young child is sent into a room where there is a toy that must not be touched. There is also a dish of candy that must not be touched. The child is then watched through a one-way mirror. Children are timed to see how long they can resist taking some candy.

In cases involving boys, all yielded to the temptation to take some candy. But some held out longer than others. In boys who resisted for an extended time, a younger boy was sent in with instructions that the candy was for him to eat--contradicting the instructions to the older boy. Older boys with "strong consciences" turned out to be those with the warmest relationships with their fathers. These would attempt to distract the younger boy, would repeat the rule as it came to them, and would successfully intercept the younger boy through that phase of the experiment.

Some girls never yielded, and the experiment had to be ended without a final measurement. The strength of resistance was measured in terms of the length of time that passed before the child would violate the rule laid down. The research findings are impressive. The resistance to temptation seems to be directly related to the strength of the father's relationship to the son. There is a strong suggestion that "the father's association with the boy, and his stress on the importance of teaching right and wrong, are important variables in producing resistance to temptation."[8]

Merton Strommen, in studies involving 2,952 Lutheran young people, found that strong family ties seemed to produce higher "belief" scores.[9] In a nationwide survey of Free Methodist high school students in 1960, I found that young people whose parents conducted regular family altar worship were active Christians at a ratio of seven to one compared to young people who came from homes where there were no family prayers.[10]

Internalizing Jesus Christ

If the ancient Hebrew father was concerned that

God's word be "in the heart" of his children, today's Christian parents may be equally concerned about how Christian values are built into the lives of their children. This goal stands at the center of almost all the carefully worded statements of objectives for Christian teaching in the church.

Just *how* this internalizing of conscience takes place remains very largely a mystery. We are continually baffled to find two children from equally good homes becoming persons quite different from each other. We, as a church, are also perplexed when we ask ourselves how we might cast an influence for good in the life of a child. But we acknowledge that children in the same family actually occupy a different *role, status,* and *value* in that family--so each experiences a different family compared to the other. What we are learning about "family systems" surely increases our understanding about children's consciences and beliefs.

We might think that if parents wish their children to internalize Christian values and beliefs as they are growing up, the most effective way to bring it about would be to bring Deity into the role of *authority* in the child's experience: "Jesus will not love you if you do that." "God will punish you if you disobey."

But there is limited research evidence to suggest that an astonishing thing may result. The child may be confused by the introduction of a third authority who, though unseen, is evidently more powerful than either of the parents. The child may want to imitate this supra-human ideal and aspire to enjoy the same status. The findings have been interpreted to suggest that such children have failed to develop a realistic sense of their own role. Furthermore, such children may grow up imagining that they are themselves "deity--above ordinary rules and regulations which apply to normal people"! These "delusions of deity" are offered as a possible explanation for the occasional tragic deviation of people with rigid religious backgrounds.[11]

Evidently God has created us in such a way that children must find their identity by idealizing an important adult human in their lives. "You must obey Daddy and Mother" is probably the most appropriate point of reference to build in the mind of the child. Internalizing Jesus Christ as the highest authority for life seems to require that the child first accept responsibility to parents. "Honor thy father and thy mother" was, after all, God's command for children. In *Parents, Kids, and Sexual Integrity* I offer a bold extension on family systems with special attention to "God's First Curriculum: Parents, Sexuality, and Intimacy."

One of the most helpful theories yet offered to help us understand what seems to occur in the development of a child's values is one developed by David Ausubel.[12] He pictures a series of orbits through which a child passes on the way to becoming an adult. The child is pictured as a "satellite" that revolves around strong centers of values--the people he most admires. Those people tend to be strongly imitated and reflected in the child's own conscience. Here are the main lines of the rather complex Ausubel model:

1. Satellization. The young child who is strongly at-

tached to the parents, idealizes them, imitates them, and is proud to be associated with them, is said to be "well satellized." That is, the circle of values is in orbit around the parents. If they are Democrat or Tory, so is the child. If dad drives a Ford, that is the only car, and so on. If Christ and the church are important to the parents, a well-satellized child will also consider them important long before they are personally understood.

2. Non-satellization. The young child who rejects the image of the parents, spites them, detests being seen with them, and does not imitate them, is said to be a non-satellizing child. The child is at loose ends and has no fixed point of reference for values. Ausubel suggests that very often this child seems to be the child who is used to showing off to other people to build up the reputation of the parents. Non-satellization may also be brought on by hostility and rejection on the part of the parents. At any rate, this child is badly warped during those early years when attitudes and values are forming. There is strong evidence that the non-satellizing child will almost certainly be in trouble with society unless there is help. Sometimes a non-satellizing child is able to adopt a temporary center--an important outside adult, such as a neighbor or a Sunday school teacher.

3. Desatellization. As the child comes into adolescence, it is important that responsibility for free choice is given. Parents may have brought on a gradual and orderly transfer of this independence, but the child gets it one way or another. Their status in the world will no longer do for the child. Status, role, and

value must be real. The teen has personal beliefs now. That is, the values are now internalized, so the teen can go through the decision-making process inside the mind. The kid no longer needs someone to make decisions for him.

4. Resatellization. Some adolescents, in the "spin off" of desatellization, move into a temporary orbit around some other magnetic pole of values. Frequently this resatellization orbits around teenage friends. All of the power of imitation you ever saw in a kindergarten child who idolized a parent may now be demonstrated in idolizing the teen world or some of its mighty heroes. An adolescent who experiences disappointment with parents as models or who discovers that they have an inadequate view of themselves and of life may resatellize briefly around temporary models. Here the church can often serve the young person well. The pastor, Sunday school teacher, or another attractive adult in the church may fill the gap for the teenager who is spinning off from parents to be independent.

At last, the independent adult is in an established personal orbit. The strongly satellizing, emerging adult proceeding through desatellization in a healthy, though sometimes dizzy way, tends to stabilize in an orbit with a guiding set of values very much like that of the original orbit with the parents. Each of us first imitates parents' values; then we feel competent to try our wings independently. Finally we have combined ideals with experience into a tough fabric of values we call our own conscience.

This sketch of the Ausubel model is, of course,

severely condensed. It does ring true, however, to much that we can observe about us. It also rings true to the old biblical proverb: "Train up a child in the way he should go: and when he is old, he will not depart from it."[13]

The role of the church

It now remains for us to ask what the church can contribute to the formation of values in the growing person. Before we suggest ways in which the church can exert its influence, perhaps we should note some of the tempting assumptions we dare not make.

We dare not assume that the church has a higher power of authority over the conscience of a child than do the parents. All parents operate under a charter of management granted to the human race by the Creator. "Honor thy father and thy mother" is not only written as law; it is also written as a necessity into the entire psychological fabric of humanity.

We dare not assume that the church can often or consistently reverse the negative values that children have acquired from their parents, as in the case of Dick and Ann Smith.

We dare not assume that the powerful influence of a child's peers can be ignored. Just as parents operate under a charter from God, which is written into humanity, we are also created for wider networks of relationships. This means that wherever human connections are made, significant influences envelop us. One's age-mates are certain to bear a strong influence in a culture where a "day's work" consists of being clustered in the same room with children of the very same age, from five years old or earlier and until age seventeen or so, when adulthood has arrived. In the church, therefore, we must first of all try to understand how God intended us to be molded, then find ways to work "with the grain" for maximum results in bringing our peer environments into the presence of Jesus and saturating everyone with the most magnetic of Christian values.

We dare not assume that adolescent hunger for independence can be adequately accounted for by calling teenagers rebellious. The path to selfhood requires that we leave father and mother in order to be our very own selves. The church must help both adolescents and parents to make this birth of independence both beautiful and orderly.

We dare not imagine that the church can match either the quantity of or the external motivation given for ideas and information presented in the public schools. The school has more time and more kinds of pressure and rewards to apply. The church must determine what the crucial concepts are that it must develop and what strategies it can use best with its limited time. And unique to the church could be the "quality of relationships" in our network systems.

With these lines of limitation drawn, however, let us turn to the larger and more creative question of what the church can do to help people acquire and improve the quality of values which guide their lives.

The church can help parents understand their role as value makers and help them fill that role more effectively. Stresses unlike those faced at any time before in the history of the human species are now pressing down on the family. Our high mobility rate--change of jobs, ease of moving cross-country--has split up the larger family of grandparents, uncles, aunts, and cousins. This larger multi-generation family tended to give a child a longer ramp for launching his own value system. The isolated family, in contrast, rarely is able to develop the image of generations-old traditions; the immediate parents have greater opportunity and greater responsibility for character formation than they had when the family was only part of a clan.

Now, grandparents and relatives are generally people whom you travel across the country to visit. This may sometimes seem to have advantages, but it does deprive the child of a larger frame of reference for establishing family values. At this same moment in our history the birthrate has been sharply cut back, and families tend to be smaller--further limiting the number of persons who stand in immediate roles of family influence.

What is more, the social patterns of American life have been gradually developing to separate the family. Whereas once our social activities were largely for families, we now tend to slice social life by age-groups. Parents have their own friends, parties, clubs, and entertainment. Adolescents have their own complete circuit of social contacts, often with few overlaps into families who are also friends of their parents. Even some pre-teens have their own social calendar.[14]

The church must keep alive the biblical and human

vision of the significance of the family. The family is the institution in which people are born and shaped and in which human relationships find their highest meaning. There is also a sense in which the fellowship of the church can fill the void left by the loss of the extended family of grandparents, uncles, aunts, and cousins. It can even furnish the important "brother" and "sister" associations so badly needed by children in the small family. Persons in the church tend to share many of the same values and may become important sources of influence to which we may expose our children.

The church must help parents understand the importance of their role in shaping the consciences of their children. The church owes parents not only that kind of information but also the additional resources to guide them in purposeful family living and family education. The churches have not moved vigorously to help the home join the Christian education team. Indeed, the emergence of the Sunday school movement and the multiplication of Christian education ministries in the local church have tended to say to the family, "We can make your children Christian; leave it to us." It now becomes one of our most urgent tasks to find ways to return to the home the initiative in the nurture of its young and the instillation of Christian values.

The church must also ask itself how its program may be changed so as to retain family solidarity. The church calendar may contribute to the breakdown of family life by age-segregation of its total program or by breaking into valuable blocks of time needed for family activities. In the interest of improving Christian education in the church we have clustered and graded children and young people until the mystery of the fellowship of the church may have been badly damaged. No doubt it is time for innovators in the church to guide us in returning from our grading and grouping spree. It is evident that we need a moderate program that contains both isolated age-group features and mixed age-group ministries if church education is to be both education and church in its results.

The church must accept the task, also, of making creative use of the adolescent need for independence. We must ask ourselves what status-giving motivation we can develop that will help to satisfy young people who need to feel that they are individuals of worth and ability. The church can also provide understanding and confidential ministries through its pastor and its workers with young people.

Teens' age-mates can be made a significant and positive influence during those years when they are looking for values among people besides their parents. Just as the church must recognize the God-given role of parents in nurture and conscience formation, so also the church must recognize the normal need for acquiring status with one's peers. Church ministries to children and youth must be creatively planned to take maximum advantage of Christian fellowship with peers. As they build strong ties of friendship, Christian values may be spread through a controlled contagion.

Throughout history the church has provided this kind of nucleus around which a person may spin off, may find a place to anchor during the time independence is being asserted and established. It was probably this kind of imitation that prompted Paul to write twice to the immature Corinthian Christians: "Be ye followers of me, even as I also am of Christ."[15] With saints in all stages of development in the church, it is important for us to remember that no person is made whole until he moves on into his own independent orbit with values derived from the living Christ who resides within him--in his heart. As we better understand the once-in-a-lifetime thirst of the adolescent to become his very own self, the church can perhaps minister with increasing effectiveness to its teen-agers.

The advantage of age-mate learning situations, which the public school enjoys, is shared by the church. Although the Sunday morning class amounts to only about one-fortieth of the time the public school has the child or teen, the same atmosphere of exploration and discovery can prevail. And the number of hours spent in a classroom is not always a measure of the impact of a class on one's life and experience. Recall, for example, from your own school experience whether there seems to be a direct relationship between the number of hours you spent in a given class and the abundance or scarcity of memories. Many a weekly college seminar has survived in the memory better than classes that met daily. The Sunday school class might be thought of as a seminar where discussion and planning and sharing of ideas are more important than mastery of facts or testing for recall. Or think of it as a laboratory where the thirst for new insight is strong, and investigation is the mode of inquiry.

We will do well to remember that the church, unlike the schools or any other institution or agency in the world, serves both the home and the peer group. People may feel that the American home cannot be brought into action to shape the future. They may speak as public school educators and do so with some credibility. The church, however, has a unique relationship to the family. Besides, it can legitimately be questioned whether human history could or would long survive if the family disappeared. Perhaps the congregation is uniquely positioned to undergird and strengthen families, since its very theology is rooted in "the image of God, male and female" whose charge and commission is to "fill the earth" with family and to give accountability to God for its creative and responsible management. So, the church should be developing programs calculated to offer encouragement, support, and new information about how to carry out this original charge from the Creator to families.

Ultimately, of course, the church seeks to confront every person with the claims of Jesus, which call us all to discipleship. All of the energies of the church bend to this effort of presenting every person as a candidate for the transforming and renewing power of Christ. A person's life is then reorganized and centered in a personal and meaningful orbit around the King of Kings and Lord of Lords.

10

A Proposal for Tomorrow

There are great hazards facing anyone who attempts to make predictions in these times. Some people claim that history repeats itself and that, therefore, it is easy to predict the future by knowing one's history. But the old assertion--which may have had an element of validity during the long centuries of man's primitive existence--is hardly adequate for today. It collapses chiefly on the fact that history cannot repeat itself; we are not feeding the same elements into it. These are new times. We know ourselves better than did any generation before. We know our environment better. Although we seem to create new and greater kinds of pain and trouble, we have tools for identifying and understanding the real nature of our problems. We hope that we are also much nearer finding solutions, too. This is not to say that a golden tomorrow is guaranteed; indeed, tomorrow may be ushered out by a wave of atomic mushrooms. Or it may be left in shambles in the wake of some insane racial genocide or some terrorist attack on a global scale. But it will be different from any previous time--and hence not easily predictable.

Although we imagine that nuclear and space developments are our greatest signs of change, it may well be that history will record of us that equally significant changes were brought on by less flamboyant discoveries. The process of education, for example, is being radically changed as we come to know human nature and human potential better. Not everyone is interested in going to the moon. Some thoughtful scientists are trying to break through into an understanding of the roots of the deeper human problems:

How to enhance the value of human life and to protect the victims of our greed and self-centered consumption and extravagance;

How to establish sexual integrity expressed exclusively in life-long, high-quality relationships;

How to identify enduring values across centuries within a species in which wisdom is acquired so slowly and often too late to influence the surging appetites of newer members of the race;

How to express those enduring values to our young.

After making the observations of the previous nine chapters, I am probably obligated to say something about their implications for the immediate future of learning in the church. I choose not to predict what shape church education will take in twenty-five years. Instead, I wish only to set down what it seems to me are desirable and possible developments.

The "Concept Curriculum"

It becomes evident that the most urgent educational ministry for people in the church is instruction that leads to the development of significant concepts. Traditional Sunday school lessons tend to be taught either as Bible events cast in interesting stories or as Bible content set forth as "ground to cover." The use of rich Bible material in either of these ways creates the impression that if we know the story or have covered the ground, we have no further need to consider the Bible material. It also suggests that the Bible is merely a book to be known, when, in fact, it is a book which must be brought to life as its grand ideas catch our vision.

It is true that certain of the key concepts require a grasp of the flow of events over a sustained period of time, so at some point a person must acquire the big picture of God's work through history. God's acts of redemption form a parallel concept that has the appearance of "ground covering." But the learner need not plow through the vast stretches of the centuries at a snail's pace in once-a-week intervals; indeed, if he did, he would almost certainly lose the big picture and be lost in a field of disconnected facts and events. Perhaps such "high altitude" concepts should be explored in a more concentrated curriculum than the once-a-week Sunday school.

Most concepts have an individuality and a complexity that make them worthy of intensive and recurring exploration. Noah, for example, might be met by students looking at the acts of God in history, but there is a great deal more to discover about him than his place in time. Suppose that in our master list of concepts worthy of exploration the concept of *grace* is included. Noah is a person of whom Scripture

141

records that he "found grace in the eyes of the Lord."[1] In developing a working definition of grace, we should carefully examine Noah's relationship to God. In fact, many young adults who have come up through Sunday school seem never to have formed the concept of grace in anything like an adequate way.

Suppose, again, that our master list of concepts worth knowing as an adult contains the concept of *perfection.* We may find ourselves going back to Noah again to discover what Scripture means when it says that Noah was perfect in his generation.[2] We will, of course, explore in depth Jesus' words in Matthew 5:48. But an adequate concept of perfect when applied to believers in God requires patient and repeated weaving together of a wide range of perceptions.

Both of these examples illustrate how a concept curriculum, whether designed by denominational curriculum planners or developed by parents for use with their own children, differs significantly from a curriculum that is planned to "cover the ground." Indeed, a concept curriculum might seem sometimes to cover very little ground and to cover it very slowly, for great ideas take time to grow. They tend to stimulate spontaneous adventures in learning, which also take time.

An immediate need is for the development of a master list of Christian education concepts focused on urgent human needs and pain. Such a listing of issues in Christian education would identify the urgent agendas, principles, and values which are of abiding concern to humankind. Age-level perceptions and developmental progressions should be defined for each of these, and a hierarchy and structure given to the entire list.[3]

The next step would require that for each concept a complete set of procedures be developed, tested, and refined for use in teaching the concept, and an "inside search" conducted to verify exactly how the learning is accomplished. Procedures would be needed for dealing with the required perceptions at each level.

The master list of concepts for Christian education must be developed by drawing on resource persons with the best competences available in psychology, sociology, anthropology, and especially biblical theology. A continuing study should be maintained as concepts are identified, defined, revised, and enlarged.

After the master list is available, the procedures should be developed by bringing to the task the best energies of learning experts and curriculum development specialists. The procedures for each concept would be carefully validated through actual teaching in pilot and research settings. And since human insight and imaginations are constantly changing with the culture, the curriculum development task is perpetual. We not only know ourselves better as we do our work, we also discover deeper realities of God through better perception of who Jesus is and what is revealed in Scripture.

These two kinds of working commissions require calling together a task force of people having scarce resources. Not many publishers could afford a panel of such people on their staffs. Besides, if the resource people are to maintain their skills, they are more likely to do so in research and educational settings than in actual materials' preparation employment. The implications then become clear. Denominational curriculum developers and publishers must turn to research and high-skill talents most often found in colleges, seminaries, and universities. These experts should be engaged for specialized services as needed, retained for short-term and long-term responsibilities, and taken into the field to verify for themselves the changing nature of human needs within a changing culture.

Today theological and social science resource people from university, college, and seminary faculties are being tapped for occasional consulting services. But ecclesiastical bodies consistently bypass college and seminary faculty members, rarely bringing them into team projects, and even more rarely recruiting or electing them for denominational leadership posts.

The research we need is rarely available from our colleges and seminaries, since great research institutions are those which have found both resources and doctoral programs through which to generate research. It seems reasonable to predict that a call for help from the curriculum developers might provide an impetus to educational research and Christian education specialization in the denominational colleges and graduate schools. In addition, the curriculum developers might act to reach research scholars, graduate students, and research specialists whose energies might be harnessed. They could contribute to the task of identifying concepts and developing the educational procedures for building them in the minds of children, young people, and adults in the church.

One of the most promising trends today is visible as various alliances of denominations extend the network of cooperative curriculum development and publication. The same trend has also sprung up within the so-called independent publishers of Sunday school and general church curriculum. Part of the impetus is economic, but a larger motivation rests on the determination to stand together in articulating the world's best hope to the widest possible markets. Some publishers are in touch regularly by telephone to consult with their client congregational leaders about needed products as well as to identify resources the congregation may need in order to cope with the devastation of living in the present age.

The "Spiral Curriculum"

Jerome Bruner of Harvard offers us an amazingly simple thesis:

Any concept worth knowing as an adult can be represented in some intellectually honest form to any person of any age. That is, there are *percepts* that may be explored within any age or ability level which contribute to building the larger *concept*.

Suppose, in our research, that we discover there are a dozen (or a hundred) concept families which have abiding significance in the life of a person, especially in equipping people to cope with change, danger, and pain in this present world. Then, these concepts need to be scheduled for exploration by every growing person periodically across his life span. Bruner

145

suggests that even the elementary child's curriculum should be tested in every point to determine whether the things learned have abiding and expanding value in the real world.[4] Bruner thinks that those things should be discarded that do not contribute in some way to the large concepts which will be useful to him as an adult.

This is not to say that a preschool or an early elementary child should be expected to deal precisely and definitively with a concept such as Christian perfection. But there are numerous perceptions we might grasp that are useful to us in childhood and in youth, and that also begin to build a foundation for a well-formed concept to sustain us as adults and eventually in old age. Our earliest insights into the concept may be represented by action or by images. Most surely we will open up our early understandings along intuitive lines more than along analytical ones. But foundational percepts of our concept of Christian perfection include (1) our perception of constant love as an attribute of parents, (2) our earliest impressions of the God who has loved us constantly and perfectly, (3) our own inward yearning for harmonious and satisfying relationships, and (4) our inclination to work for closure--completed tasks and full-blown ideas, for example. These begin to lay a base for an increasingly well-focused idea of God's image restored through the grace of Jesus Christ in people who are recreated and made whole in the image of God's Son.

By calling for a *spiral curriculum* I am only urging that the concepts our students need should be ar-

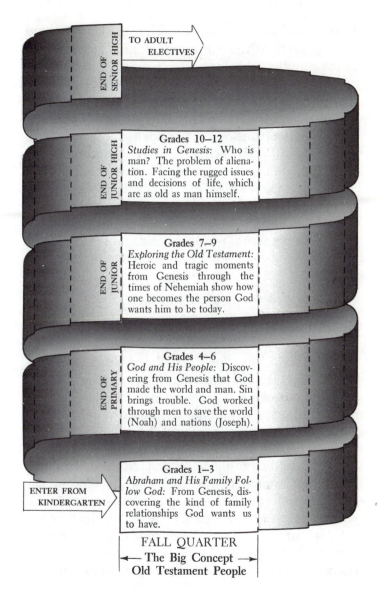

END OF SENIOR HIGH

TO ADULT ELECTIVES →

END OF JUNIOR HIGH

Grades 10–12
Studies in Genesis: Who is man? The problem of alienation. Facing the rugged issues and decisions of life, which are as old as man himself.

END OF JUNIOR

Grades 7–9
Exploring the Old Testament: Heroic and tragic moments from Genesis through the times of Nehemiah show how one becomes the person God wants him to be today.

END OF PRIMARY

Grades 4–6
God and His People: Discovering from Genesis that God made the world and man. Sin brings trouble. God worked through men to save the world (Noah) and nations (Joseph).

ENTER FROM KINDERGARTEN →

Grades 1–3
Abraham and His Family Follow God: From Genesis, discovering the kind of family relationships God wants us to have.

FALL QUARTER
← The Big Concept →
Old Testament People

ranged mechanically for recurring exploration and development. At the minimum, a spiral curriculum for the Sunday school would schedule these concepts not only for an orderly progression along a horizontal time plane but also for orderly repetition of concept exploration at the higher levels. Timing and spacing should be determined by the span of the age-level cycles, presumably bringing each concept up for additional exploration during the span of each cycle. I have suggested earlier that the traditional grouping of preschool, early elementary, upper elementary, junior high, and senior high age-groups seems both to serve developmental purposes and to offer sufficient breadth for a comprehensive coverage of essential concepts.

Closing the generation gap

If it is true, as the Cornell research seems to suggest, that the American society is pulling apart at the peer culture seams,[5] church education ministries might find ways of helping to mend the tear in our culture. A distinctive feature of the Judeo- Christian strain in history has been its vision that the home is the fountainhead of moral and spiritual values and instruction in a particular lifestyle. The Cornell research found that Russian peer groups serve the national interest in shaping children's values by social pressure. This socialistic model of conscience development is particularly well suited in a culture where a rapid change in mass viewpoint and values is wanted. Both the Judeo-Christian and the demo-cratic view of humanity have been that we are obli-gated to our own history. We have held that long-treasured values are not quickly erased from the minds of any people without jeopardizing the future of humanity. Hence, these viewpoints have tended to hold the family in high regard as the custodian of values, in contrast to the more laboratory-like situ-ation in which a government or a particular leader imposes a new set of values by applying peer and political pressure according to personal, economic, or insane whims.

It may be of profound importance, therefore, that we find ways of restoring the initiative for moral instruction to the American home. A major problem confronting our best efforts, however, is the substan-tial decline in traditional "father-mother-children" households. We will find ourselves having to be flex-ible in order to serve single parent homes, separating families, and blended families in addition to the simpler "nuclear household" we have long held up as our model. In the proposal I am making there are two specific kinds of action that seem to be open to us in closing the generation gap as we focus on families.

One potential solution is in creating family time together models and demonstrating them in mag-netic ways. Such time together deserves a light cur-riculum of experiences, conversation starters, and games to provide family leaders with some basic agendas. Perhaps only parents who have a high interest in the Christian nurture of their children will respond to such a program, but then parents who make commitments to Jesus and the church tend to be those who want to be the best parents. With a generation of biblically naive adults now with us, having removed Bible stories and narratives from public schools so long ago, we cannot assume that today's parents are at home with Bible material. "I need to go to Janie's class," one young mother confided. "I'm embarrassed to go to an adult class because I will likely feel so stupid. I don't know anything."

With a spiral curriculum, which gives recurring attention to the great issues, principles, and values of the Christian faith, a home curriculum can serve a great mission. By careful timing in the church study schedule, all age levels can be exploring within the same concept area at the same time. At home there can then be reinforcing conversations on the common concept. Two benefits are obvious: (1) Parents, the most significant people in the lives of children, have an opportunity to speak on the most important issues of life in the presence of their children. Many parents would welcome that opportunity, but few have the initiative to create their own religious education program. Consequently, in the harried and stratified family life of our culture, many children never hear their parents speak on the issues of faith and life. (2) Children join the education team as they contribute to conversations in which other children are forming ideas. It is no secret that a twelve-year-old can often make clear to a six-year-old things which a parent gropes helplessly to explain. The modes of representation evidently are more similar among children themselves than between children and adults. What is more, the values of an idolized big brother or sister go a long way in influencing a younger child in the family. A home and family curriculum brings all these influences to bear on the formation of values. The curriculum can follow a daily dinner-table devotional and discussion format or can be arranged for an extended evening or Sunday afternoon session the family chooses to set aside.

Parents must also understand that a formal religious curriculum at home is not all-sufficient. The hidden or "phantom curriculum" of any household is spun out in the day-by-day attitudes and opinions expressed by parents. Perhaps the home curriculum can help to keep this phantom dimension more intentional in the minds of parents. Without dictating its content, guidelines might help them see the potential power of their own viewpoints on moral issues, of their behavior under stress, and of their attitudes toward other people both within the home and outside it.

A second way of consolidating the generations through Christian education ministries in the church would involve temporary but periodic breaking down of the airtight age-level groupings in the church. Again, with a concept curriculum arranged in a timed spiral, we could deliberately shuffle people to spread their ideas. For example, selected junior high young people could help for two or three Sundays in the primary classes. There they could participate in discovery and in conversations having a bearing on the concept being explored. Or we could bring selected families together for three sessions to share insights and do further exploration together on the concept being considered. It is conceivable that in a given church, traditional groups above the junior level might be suspended for three weeks. All of the constituency might be engaged systematically in seminars for the whole family, in instructional assistance in young children's classes, or in cross-generation exploration seminars grouped for specialized or intensive work. Such a restructuring of the classes would provide a potentially exciting culmination to a period of exploration with one's own peers. At the same time it would tend to cement the entire church community as the flow of common concepts spread across the generations. Senior teens can surely lead or entertain the senior adults, or both, to communicate cross-culturally how the rule of God works in their world. And Senior adults would serve the teens well to return the favor. Intergenerational *bonding* is critical if we are to conserve the wisdom of the aging and energize the rest of us with the considerable vigor of the young. The pastor's pulpit role in all of this across-the-life-cycle curriculum might be open to equally creative innovation.

Programmed instruction in the church

Programmed instruction refers to the use of teaching techniques or devices that provide the learner with a series of learning steps, each of which is rewarded if properly completed. The so-called teaching machine is one form of programmed instruction.

The typical machine presents a small piece of information that must be learned before you can proceed to the next *frame*. The reward may consist of candy, money, or simply the satisfaction of having a right answer.

Two factors combine that tend to reduce the usefulness of programmed instruction for the church. First, the church possesses a large body of ideas or concepts that it wishes to convey to the young and to the newly recruited; programmed instruction is more easily adapted for use with highly factual bodies of information than with concepts. Second, the church tends to rely upon interpersonal dialogue as the most effective means of developing those ideas or concepts in the minds of its adherents; programmed instruction tends to be most useful for individual, often solo study.

This is not to say, however, that concepts cannot be programmed or arranged for reinforcement learning. Indeed, United States servicemen subjected to Communist "education" in Korea gave us a vivid demonstration that ideas can be shaped by indoctrination accompanied by a system of rewards and punishment. But Russian psychology, which first gave us the conditioned response theory and the assumption that higher order learning was essentially the same as that of Pavlov's dogs, is reported to be turning to more active symbolical approaches to problem solving among children. At the same time American psychologists tend to be hanging on to the Pavlovian notions.[6]

Since we will want to keep alive the highest respect for the individual in all church eduation, we will not be likely to use the relatively closed system of mental manipulation in developing the grand concepts of the Christian faith. At the same time we are obligated to examine our instructional tasks to see whether there are not some that could better be handled by programmed learning. What are the heavy informational parts of our teaching ministry? What are the factual understandings which underlie the formation of our concepts?

Consider, for example, that large numbers of people come into the fellowship of the church with virtually no religious training in their childhood background. They enter their respective classes on a Sunday morning without basic information or frames of reference badly needed to participate meaningfully in the class. Computer software is now available for many basic Bible learning and Bible study tasks. But since the best programmed education applications are for foundational issues, they probably need to be custom programmed for a congregation or a particular denomination's use. Here are basic, generic kinds of programmed learning packages or software programs we could use:

Names and categories of Bible books
Condensed history of Bible events
Compact "tree" of Bible people
Denominational history
Basic beliefs: catechism

Such programs could be developed into small sections for fitting into bits of time available before public services. A system of appropriate rewards could be developed. The programs could be planned so that when one was mastered adequately it would lead to another.

There might be other uses for such programs. Children and young people enrolled in the regular ministries of the church might use them at intervals to find whether their mastery of certain understandings was progressing satisfactorily. Then, too, the performance one showed in the programs might have a bearing upon his placement in classes or in other phases of the ministry of the church.

We might adopt a guiding principle that any highly compact and precise kind of information the church wishes to teach should be considered for programmed instruction. We would program it out of respect for the energies of the student and also to conserve limited class time for the kinds of learning which require interaction, discussion, and the formation of complicated attitudes, values, and understandings. But we will want to resist placing any human being in an isolated learning program that is self-taught, self-scored, and self-administered. Christian education is, like the Creation, necessarily relational. "It is not good that Adam should be alone" applies continuously to all of us. So let us promise ourselves that we will administer education that is profoundly oriented toward creating community and enhancing the quality of human life by working with everyone in groups.

"Live Curriculum" for an adult elective

Among the most restless people in the church are those young adults neither caught yet by the concerns of parenthood nor trapped by their own childhood. These are creative and energetic individuals whose commitment to Christ thrusts them forward to create a better world. Indeed, there are many adults who fully sense their parental responsibilities and are at the same time searching urgently for some means of dealing realistically and meaningfully with the problems of their times.

A large number of young adults want to bring their own times and situations into focus in the light of the Bible and of the revelation of God in Christ. But it is not easy for a publisher to bring out curriculum materials that get at the issues of demonstrations, assassinations, riots, and campus sit-ins as they are occurring. The curriculum can speak to the perennial needs of humankind, of course, but cannot deal with the volatile, earthshaking issues and events. By the time the discussion guides get into print, the event will have long passed and the issue will have probably become vastly more complicated.

The typical Sunday school lesson is outlined and sent on its way to manuscript preparation about four years ahead of its use in a class. Publishers who operate with short deadlines still require that lesson manuscripts be in hand one year ahead of use. And when one thinks of all of the complicated supporting media needed for the vast array of curriculum one publisher puts together, it is easy to understand the need for long-range planning and scheduling.

It must be asked, however, whether a single discussion guide could not be released "live" to the thoughtful and energetic adult classes that demand to know how they can relate Jesus' concern to the complicated social and moral climate of their times. Consider the fact that live television can now take us into a hut in the remotest village in the world and that this morning's news, complete with pictures, will be printed and in the hands of millions of people tonight. One could easily ask what motivations have pushed the secular society to act with such vigor in mass and instant circulation of information and viewpoint. But if we dared to ask that question, we would also have to ask why Christian motivation to share information and interpretation of events remains content with virtually no instant means of communication. Even some denominational news magazines work with about a one-hundred day blackout time between the editors and their readers.

Let me propose that a creative team of Christian education specialists could prepare, on a week-by-week basis, a discussion guide. It might be only four pages geared to current issues and concerns to which Christian adults might address themselves. The format could incorporate reprinted news excerpts, probing questions that Christians must ask of their own history and of their own consciences. There could be citations to biblical resources and insights leading to action. This "Living Issues" adult curriculum could be compiled for a given week within a forty-eight-hour period and quick printed from typescript and stripped news excerpts. The whole thing could be ready for mailing within four days from conception. Multiple copies could be sent by overnight express or by fax. A special subscription rate could be devised for single copies, which would be specially prepared for photo-copying at the point of use. This proposal has many potential variations. I offer it here chiefly to illustrate that in the church we have not yet taken advantage of our communications technology to spur the church to action or to shape its conscience rapidly. Yet we live in an era in which powerful forces are at work to change our values and commitments.

A formula for meaningful teaching

I have brought you to the end of this book without having offered simple solutions to complex and un-usual opportunities which confront us. I have tried to illustrate the need for creative and discovery-ori-ented teaching in the church and to give illustrations that inspire both excitement and hope that learning in the church can become more meaningful for all of us.

Let me close by suggesting what may seem to be an overly simple formula that you may apply to any learning session. I have reduced it to four key words. You may find better ones, but these form a chain that, it seems to me, is particularly strong in helping to bring about meaningful learning. The four key words are *intersect, investigate, infer,* and *implement.* Here is how they interlock in a teaching-learning session:

Learning requires that the path of a student's interest is brought to *intersect* with a given idea, concept, or body of information. We sometimes speak glibly about attention-getting devices. As a last resort, such devices are instruments to intersect student interest. More powerful intersection occurs when the needs of the person are met directly by the learning experience. We always ask: What are the living concerns of these students? What are their deepest needs? What do they think their deepest needs are? Can I lead them from the supposed need to the real one? What events in their immediate environment can I capitalize on in order to lead them to significant learning? Who are their heroes? How can I bring their devotion to those heroes to intersect with a higher call to commitment? Can this concept or this body of information be organized in such a way that it is relevant to the needs and experiences of these particular students? So, for the curriculum developer, the writer, and the teacher, there is always this first claim: What we teach must first be set on a collision course to *intersect* with the awareness and interest of the person who needs to learn. If we take seriously our hypothesis that any concept worth possessing can be taught in some intellectually honest way to any child at any age, then we must find the intellectually honest way to represent the concept to the student so as to have obvious personal meaning.

Once the learner has intersected with the gold mine route leading to the rewarding concept, he needs help to *investigate* and work the rich conceptual field. If we follow discovery as a principal mode of inquiry, we will lead learners to the resources and ask them to form tentative rules or hypotheses, test them, and arrive at working principles. They will probe, explore, unmask, and synthesize their findings in the act of discovery. We will moderate the learning experience, but rarely dictate. We will question the learners, helping them to test the integrity of their hypotheses and to determine whether they have asked appropriate questions of the best resources. If they are satisfied with a weak or erroneous hypothesis, we will cite them to further resources. Investigation thus becomes the principal phase of the learning formula for the acquisition of new information and for processing it into working principles. Notice, however, that what I am proposing differs radically from either an authoritarian or a covering-the-ground strategy of teaching. At the same time, biblical resources come in for maximum use, not so much as anecdotal material, but as the source of ultimate authority for life and experience. Thus, Bible material is not encountered repeatedly in story form, but it becomes the mining field in which concepts take shape and working principles are formed. It is reasonable to believe every issue under exploration will lead ultimately and significantly to a serious examination of Bible material. Finally, the investigation will lead to formation of new *insight*--a working hypothesis or rule growing out of the collision of God's truth with the student's real life. Insight is not an activity; it is a product of intersection and investigation.

When the learners have intersected with learning and have proceeded to investigate the resources available to them, their third obligation in meaningful learning is to *infer*--to draw inferences from their findings that they can apply to real life. Here the teacher helps them to ask the critical questions: What are the implications of this finding for my day-to-day life? What generalizations can I derive from this particular concept as I have defined it? Whereas the investigative operation may often follow a convergent kind of thinking, the inferential operation requires abundant use of divergent thinking. Christian values can be applied to changing cultures only if imagination, insight, and creativity are brought to bear upon interpreting fixed principles and translating them for unpredictable situations.

Once inferences have been made and implications defined, it then remains for the learner to *implement* those understandings in actual practice. We indulge in a dangerous practice if we stop short of implementation in any learning experience in the church. If we stop with investigation, we have merely tasted of knowledge for the sake of knowledge. If we stop with inference, we have contented ourselves with being diagnosticians. Each of us who is related in any way to the educational ministry of the church must finally ask himself, for every learning event, "To what extent does this session, or this exploratory activity, bring the learners into a position to actively put their understanding to work?" It is a dangerous error for us to suppose that since we are concerned with teaching moral truth we cannot be expected to develop performance skills. Indeed, it could be successfully argued that one does not, in fact, possess moral truth unless its impact is demonstrated in the quality of life and behavior which follows.

Now, having set forth this formula for effective teaching, I will close by relating it to other concepts introduced in this set of essays and to some of the classic kinds of learning that have long been recognized. Let me first ask that you examine this model of "Life-Changing Learning." Afterward I will comment on other related ideas.

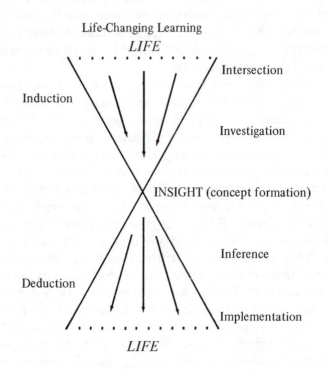

Notice that the learning experiences of our learners begin when real life is intersected by new concepts. These ideas may come from some source outside of themselves or even from their stumbling upon some message right in their environment. As they process their observations, investigate the evidence, and form tentative rules (hypotheses) that will help them make sense of the new observations in relation to their old ones, they arrive finally at *insight*. Insight comes only after they have sorted, discarded, and refined their rules until they have found the best hypothesis for dealing with this new information and all of their old understandings. From this moment on, they must live with new understanding. If they are honest, they must draw inferences from the new insight. This leads, inevitably, to changes in behavior in their lives. The quality of living is changed. When they behave differently, we may say that they have implemented their learning.

Take an example: Suppose that I am the product of an essentially Caucasian, American culture. I grow up near an Indian reservation. From my earliest infancy I have heard people say that Indians are lazy, that they drink heavily, and that, in short, they are no good. My feeling for Indians is well fixed before I even start to school; my attitudes are well developed before I think about Jesus' claim on my life. I may even be converted and still hold the same opinions about Indians; nothing in the religious life of my church directly reminds me of Indians--except references by missionaries to the residents of India, which they carefully avoid calling "Indians." Those in India are remote from me, are in desperate poverty, and need my compassion. But it is just here that I am confronted with a problem. Intersecting my peaceful life is a teaching: "God . . . has made of one blood all nations of people ..." (Acts 17:24,26). There is also the intersecting of a troubling Christian idea: All people are persons of worth to God and must be regarded as such by Christians. These collide with my own long-standing ideas and practices. At last, I see that I must rearrange the furniture of my mind and my conscience: Indians in my community are objects of God's affection. I must show the love of Jesus in my relationships with them and invest my energy in ministering to their needs.

When I pass the point of *insight,* I am then confronted with further implications of my understanding. I infer these from what I have tested and found to be reality in developing my insight. I have never cultivated the friendship of an Indian; that must change. I have never tried to see things from an Indian's point of view--history, values, culture, for example; my task is clearly growing.

At each stage of the learning experience I must decide whether I will move into the next. But no decision is more crucial than the final one. Will I act on the understanding with all of its implications for me as I understand them at the present time? Implementation is the test of effective learning; it also is the lifelong task of the learner, who must live out ever changing understandings on many hundreds of concepts.

I have suggested in the model that the top portion of the diagram represents inductive reasoning. With induction, we begin with the understandings, feelings, actions, and issues as they really are. But we add ingredients that will bring learners' attention to focus

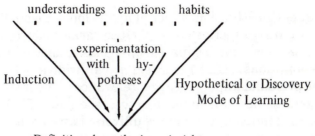

on a certain kind of problem. They will then find themselves having to cope with the problem or idea by using their previously acquired equipment--their ideas, emotions, and habits. As they stir in the new information and respond to new curiosities, they are trapped into making judgments or ground rules to cope with the new mixture they are now dealing with. They narrow their hypotheses until the best one emerges: the definition or insight.

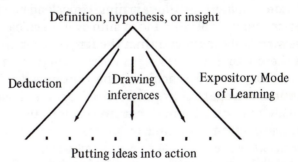

The lower portion of the "Life-Changing Learning" model represents deductive processes. With deduction we take an idea or hypothesis and work it over to get its message for us--we deduce its applications.

Our entire attention is caught by the idea. We push it down in all directions to apply it to various aspects of life. If teaching begins here, it makes one of two assumptions: (1) The learners are all wide awake to the profound importance and relevance of the insight about to be expounded for their benefit. (2) The insight, in itself, commands universal attention and banishes all other competing needs of the listeners. Either of the assumptions leaves us open to the comic tragedy of the Greek philosopher who loved to close his eyes while addressing his students--the more to follow his interesting train of thought. But alas, when he opened his eyes, he often found that he was left alone.

I have proposed the inductive-deductive model to represent life-changing learning in an effort to help us avoid the perils surrounding both modes of inquiry. The peril of induction or the hypothetical mode of inquiry *when used alone* is that it may lead nowhere in particular. It assumes that man by himself can find his way, and that man by himself can discover all that he needs to know. The peril of deduction or the expository mode of teaching is that *when used alone* it tends to disregard the real needs of learners, seems to ignore the fundamental nature of man and of the processes of learning, and, in short, may be answering questions which are not being asked by the learners.

In the educational work of the church we are committed to the view that if man is to find his way, it will be by the grace and wisdom of God. This means that the "what if" mode of inquiry is always carried out in such a way as to bring to light ultimate evidences. All learners are accepted where they are with the needs they possess, but evidences from the revelation of God in Jesus Christ and Holy Scripture are injected into their experiences as they begin to formulate a meaningful pattern for themselves. For example, we use the ultimate truth, not to bludgeon our "woman of Samaria" to death, but to dissolve the shackles of her ignorance, superstition, and sin so as to open to her the vision of what she was meant to be. What is more, finding her where she is with the real needs she possesses, we furnish the percepts only as she can take them in. The concept is what she builds from them. She did it, but not by herself. We entered her perceptual field--her real life as she saw it--and expanded her vision by injecting evidences leading to ultimate truth. The Spirit of God and of truth thus grants both the message and the insight in the mystery of learning in the church.

The point at which the two triangles meet in the "Life-Changing Learning" model represents discovery that is more than human discovery. It represents the insight that comes when we have wrestled to reconcile what we already knew with what we have found to best serve the ultimate reality--God's revelation of himself in Jesus Christ and in Holy Scripture. The *intersection* is always a confrontation of life as it is with clues about life as it may become. Thus *insight* always gives us a hypothesis that has the dimensions both of human experience and of God's grace.

From this point on, we are ready for exploration in the expository mode. What are the implications of this insight for me? What can I infer from what I have understood and experienced? We met our candidate where she was (Life=Samaria); she then formulated a hypothesis about what she might become. It now becomes important for her to know the implications of all of this for now (Life=Samaria). Definitions become important to her when she has advanced to the level of asking for meanings; they might have had no interest to her before she felt the restlessness awakened by the claims of Christ upon her. By the grace and power of God she can then put into action the new understandings she has about herself.

Thus, the "Life-Changing Learning" model combines the hypothetical and the expository modes of inquiry for the special purposes of Christian education. Such education respects both the dilemma of people as they are and the authority and vitality of the Christian revelation as the vision which transforms them. We are able, in this way, to imitate our Lord, who always began with life as it is in order to help a person discover what it ought to be. Our traditional limited "expository mode" has probably been the product of laziness; we were not so attentive to Jesus' method with people as we were to grasp and proclaim the essence of what He taught.

In this model we may have achieved the best of two possible worlds. We have found the learners where they are and have planted seeds of discontent and renewal that will help them begin their discovery of their real needs and appropriate solutions. When they have discovered those solutions, have felt the vibration of their ring of truth, we can then help them to find the definitions and the implications for turning their knowledge into action in their world. Perhaps there is no more concise description of meaningful learning in the church.

Notes

1. What's Going On in Sunday School?

[1]Russell Bennett, "Measurement of Pupil Bible Knowledge in Selected Baptist Sunday Schools in Kentucky," unpublished thesis, Southern Baptist Theological Seminary, Louisville, Kentucky, 1957. For an example of the popular type, see "Key Looks at the Sunday School," *Key to Christian Education,* 7:1-5, Fall, 1968.

[2]Informal survey carried out by the author in religious education conferences sponsored by the United States Air Force for Protestant chapel staffs in England, Germany, Turkey, and Spain, January 30 through March 5, 1968. If "Paul Revere" had been accepted as a correct answer to question 2, the mean would have been raised from 6.3 percent to 15.9 percent. Only one young airman, a college graduate in history, "correctly" answered No. 2 with "John Dawes," noting that although Revere began the ride, he was captured and taken out to sea on a British ship. Most respondents said they had never heard of Dawes, but they had memorized Longfellow. Today, historians have evidence that Samuel Prescott was actually the first to reach Concord with the news. It was a trick question, not unlike some "trade secrets" around theological or churchly fine points we like to hold like clout over the naive.

[3]One critic has made the radical proposal that volunteer and lay teachers should no longer be allowed to teach religious truths. He proposes abandoning the traditional Sunday school and having the ministerial staff of every church conduct religious education classes during available time throughout the week. See Wesner Fallaw, *Church Education for Tomorrow* (Philadelphia: The Westminster Press, 1960), 215 pp.

[4]My commitment on these basic concepts is reflected in what one of my friends has lavishly called "a pre-primer in theology," *The Holy Spirit and You* (New York: Abingdon, 1965).

2. Focus on People

[1]Lois E. Le Bar probes this principle in Jesus' teaching in an insightful way in *Education That Is Christian* (Westwood, New Jersey: Fleming H. Revell Company, 1958), p. 56ff. In her most recent book, *Focus on People* (Westwood, New Jersey: Fleming H. Revell Company, 1968), Dr. LeBar expresses concerns that are somewhat related to those of this chapter. She explores the "focus" in its implications for administration and organization in the church education ministry. I have gone, instead, into an exploration of the nature of human needs, which, it seems to me, is the fundamental theological issue we must face if Christian education is to be *education*.

[2]John 10:10, *New English Bible.*

[3]Abraham H. Maslow, *Motivation and Personality,* ch. V (New York: Harper & Row, Publishers, 1954).

[4]Matthew 25:42, *New English Bible.*

[5]James 2:15-16, *New English Bible.*

[6]Maslow, p. 94.

[7]Colossians 1:28.

3. People, Wholeness, and Holiness

[1]Dorothy Sayers, *The Man Born to Be King* (New York: Harper & Row, Publisher, 1943), p. 178.

[2]Matthew 23:15 *(New English Bible).* E. Mansell Pattison has commented on the apparent tendency of "Fundamentalistic" churches to warp personality. See his popularly written "Closed Mind Syndrome," *Christian Medical Society Journal,* Spring, 1966, pp. 7-11. See also his unpublished address to the American Association for the Advancement of Science (Berkeley, 1965), "The Effects of a Religious Culture's Values on Psychotherapy."

[3]Donald M. Joy, *The Holy Spirit and You* (New York: Abingdon, 1965), p. 38.

[4]Carl R. Rogers, *On Becoming a Person* (Boston: Houghton Mifflin Company, 1961), p. 166.

[5]John 10:10, *New English Bible.*

[6]John 4:1-26.

[7]Ephesians 4:24.

[8]Ephesians 4:24 and Colossians 3:10.

[9]Romans 8:29.

[10]This checklist is essentially a biblical one, but I was inspired to compile it after studying what is referred to as "the perceptual theory of human personality" as set forth by Arthur W. Combs and the late Donald Snygg in *Individual Behavior* (New York: Harper and Row, 1959).

[11]Matthew 19:19.

[12]Philippians 4:13, *Today's English Version.*

[13]Combs and Snygg, p. 242.

[14]II Corinthians 4:7-9, *New English Bible.*

[15]C. S. Lewis, *Mere Christianity* (New York: The Macmillan Company, 1958), pp. 172-173.

[16]Joy, p.32.

[17]Romans 12:2, *The New Testament in Modern English* by J. B. Phillips (New York: The Macmillan Company, 1958). Used by permission.

4. Can I Teach a Million Facts?

[1]The graph is based upon the findings of Ebbinghaus and reported by him in 1885. Most modern psychology textbooks cite his studies and carry this and other graphs based upon them.

[2]"Perception" as I have used it corresponds to the cognitive operation called "cognition" by J. P. Guilford in "Three Faces of Intellect," *American Psychologist,* August, 1959, pp. 469-479.

[3]G. A. Miller, "The Magical Number Seven, Plus or Minus Two," *Psychological Review,* No. 63, 1956, pp. 81- 97.

[4]The list from Matthew 10:2-4 is as follows:

Simon (Peter)	Thomas
Andrew	Matthew
James	James (of Alpheus)
John	Lebbeus (Thaddeus)
Philip	Simon (Canaanite)
Bartholomew	Judas Iscariot

See also Mark 3:16-19; Luke 6:14-16; and Acts 1:13 for other listings.

[5]See Jerome S. Bruner's chapter "The Importance of Structure" in *The Process of Education* (New York: Alfred A. Knopf, Inc., 1960), pp. 17-32.

[6]David Ausubel, in *The Psychology of Meaningful Verbal Learning* (New York: Grune and Stratton, 1963), calls this process of filing, rearranging, and growing of information the process of "subsumption." As we subsume a fact, we absorb it into the cognitive structure growing in our minds.

5. To Memorize or Not

[1]For a discussion of the requisites for memorization, see Robert M. Gagne's chapter, "Chaining: Motor and Verbal," *The Conditions of Learning* (New York: Holt, Rinehart, and Winston, Inc., 1965), pp. 87-112.

[2]David S. Warner, ed., *Arnold's Practical Sunday School Commentary*, 1919 (Chicago: Fleming H. Revell Company, 1918), p. 160, lesson for September 7, 1919.

6. Acquiring the Really Big Ideas

[1]Cf. ch. 4, "Can I Teach a Million Facts?" p.55.

[2]Cf. ch. 1, "What's Going On in Sunday School?" p.20.

[3]Experimental study by the author, "Effectiveness of Transfer of Moral Values in Classroom Instruction compared to Home Instruction," in progress during winter, 1968-1969.

[4]Acts 9:6, *New King James Version.*

[5]Acts 9:20, *New English Bible.*

7. Knowing by Feeling What You Do

[1]Mary Elizabeth Sergent, "Why Aren't They Like Us?" *The Christian Century,* October 3, 1962, pp. 1191-1194. Copyright 1962 Christian Century foundation. Paraphrased by permission.

[2]I am referring here to Jerome Bruner's "modes of representation." For simplicity I am calling his "enactive representation" merely "action learning"; "iconic" becomes "image"; and "symbolic" is rendered simply by "words." For a discussion of his ideas see Jerome Bruner, *Toward a Theory of Instruction* (Cambridge: Harvard University Press, 1966), pp. 10-14.

[3]Hebrews 1:1-3, *New English Bible.*

8. Teaching for Decision Making

[1]Joy P. Guilford, in "Three Faces of Intellect" *(Ameri-*

can Psychologist, 14:469-479, August 1959), has given us a useful model of human intellect. He uses the model to suggest that there are a series of cognitive *contents* (figural, symbolic, semantic, and behavioral), which interact with another dimension representing cognitive *products* (units, classes, relations, systems, transformations, and implications). The model is in the form of a cube. A third dimension completes the multiplied kinds of combinations that are possible. It is called cognitive *operations.* These operations are cognition, memory, convergent thinking, divergent thinking, and evaluation. I have used his list of operations to explore the various kinds of thinking that we may cultivate in the Christian education setting.

[2]See ch. 5, "To Memorize or Not," p. 66ff.

[3]John 14:6; John 8:32.

[4]Colossians 1:15-17, *New English Bible.*

[5]Colossians 2:3, *New English Bible.*

[6]Shirley H. Engle, "Decision Making: The Heart of Social Studies Instruction," *Social Education,* 24:301- 304, 306, November, 1960.

9. How Are Values Formed?

[1]See the opening anecdote in ch. 7.

[2]Shirley H. Engle, p. 301.

[3]See ch. 7, "Knowing by Feeling What You Do," p.92.

[4]See Urie Bronfenbrenner, "The Split-Level American Family," *Saturday Review,* Vol. L., No. 40:60-66, October 7, 1967.

[5]James S. Coleman, *The Adolescent Society* (New York: The Free Press, 1961), pp. 4, 173-219.

[6]Current research project by the author, "Effectiveness of Transfer of Moral Values in Classroom Instruction Compared to Home Instruction."

[7]See ch. 7, "Knowing by Feeling What You Do," p. 85.

[8]R.R. Sears and others, *Identification and Childrearing* (Stanford: Stanford University Press, 1965), p. 231.

[9]Merton Strommen, *Profiles of Church Youth* (St. Louis: Concordia, 1963).

[10]Donald M. Joy, "A Survey and Analysis of the Experiences, Attitudes, and Problems of Senior High Youth of the Free Methodist Church," unpublished thesis, Southern Methodist University, August, 1960.

[11]See E. Mansell Pattison's discussion of some recent

research and the inferences he makes in "The Effects of a Religious Culture's Values on Psychotherapy," unpublished address to the American Association for the Advancement of Science (Berkeley, 1965), p. 21.

[12]David Ausubel, *Theory and Problems of Adolescent Development* (New York: Grune and Stratton, 1954), pp. 167-216.

[13]Proverbs 22:6.

[14]See Bronfenbrenner article for an excellent exploration of this stratification.

[15]I Corinthians 11:1; cf. also 4:16.

10. A Proposal for Tomorrow

[1]Genesis 6:8

[2]Genesis 6:9

[3]Three useful lists cataloging learners' basic needs, learners' engagement in the learning tasks, and possible results of learning are incorporated in *Tools of Curriculum Development for the Church's Educational Ministry* (Anderson, Indiana: Warner Press, Inc., 1967), pp. 23-70. A list of "concepts" would differ somewhat from even the third of these and especially would need the additional classifica-

tion indicating both the logical and the urgency order of the many concepts. And no taxonomy has been generated that is composed of urgent human needs and their interface with Holy Scripture.

[4]Jerome Bruner, *The Process of Education* (New York: Random House, Inc., 1960), p. 52.

[5]See discussion in ch. 9, pp. 111, 112. See also Urie Bronfenbrenner, "The Split-Level American Family," *Saturday Review,* Vol. L., No. 40:60-66, October 7, 1967.

[6]Jerome Bruner, in "The Act of Discovery," *On Knowing: Essays for the Left Hand* (New York: Atheneum, 1965), p. 92.

INDEX